HOW TO DESIGN

YOUR DREAM HOME

(IN 25 YEARS OR LESS!)

JAN JONES EVANS

How to Design Your Dream Home (In 25 Years or Less!)
Copyright © 2022 by Jan Jones Evans

ISBN:	Paperback:	978-1-63945-463-1
	Hardcover:	978-1-63945-465-5
	Ebook:	978-1-63945-464-8

Writers' Branding 1800-608-6550
www.writersbranding.com
orders@writersbranding.com

DEDICATION

To Rick Evans, my wonderful, loving husband of 37 years, who put up with my creative bent over the years. His patience endured through the construction or renovation of four of our five marital homes.

To Mary Rawlins Ramzel, my best friend, who has put up with reviewing my thousands of floor plan ideas over the years and pretended to be interested. She even inspired some of my best ideas!

To my children and anyone else who would listen, for getting excited with me as I came up with more ideas for what our "dream home" could be like.

To my brother, Rick Jones, who encouraged me to write about my adventures and experiences through the years while designing and building my dream home, and to market my "awesome" floor plan (according to him).

To our builder, Mark Welch, who truly made our dreams come true – and then some!

In memory of my parents, Bill and Adelle Jones, who made me who I am and inspired my love of home, family and "The American Dream" of home ownership.

Contents

Chapter One — Introduction.. 1

Chapter Two — Layout And Design 11

Chapter Three — Size Does Matter!.............................. 39

Chapter Four — Location! Location! Location!............................ 47

Chapter Five — The Nitty Gritty: Foundation And Utilities 51

Chapter Six — Building, Materials, And "Going Green".............. 59

Chapter Seven — Lighting, Electrical, And Technology.............. 69

Chapter Eight — Doors, Windows, And Fire Exits...................... 77

Chapter Nine — Handicapped Accessible? 87

Chapter Ten — The Kitchen 91

Chapter Eleven — Bathrooms And Laundry 113

Chapter Twelve — Storage, Closets, And Cabinets 125

Chapter Thirteen — Décor/Design/Color/Finishing............... 137

Chapter Fourteen — Garage, Porches, And Outside Areas 145

Chapter Fifteen — Remodelling.................................. 151

Chapter Sixteen — My Floor Plan 153

CHAPTER ONE

INTRODUCTION

In the Spring of 1986, my husband and I were out camping at our favorite spot in the Missouri Ozarks at Table Rock Lake. The weather had turned cold and gray, so we decided to go into town for a change of scenery. We were walking down the plaza, window shopping along the way, when we came to a real estate office. There, front and center, was a breathtaking picture of a lake front lot with Dogwood trees in full bloom. We were hooked. We went in the office right then and there and asked if we could see that very property.

We signed a contract that afternoon and closed a couple of months later, without even looking at any other properties. We felt like we suddenly owned a piece of heaven! We had always intended to someday build our retirement home at the lake, so now we had taken the first step. I think I began sketching floor plan ideas before we ever even got home from that camping trip.

That was in 1986. In the Spring of 2011 (25 years later), we were retired and living in that lake house! Awesome doesn't begin to describe the experience of building the house that I created from my own imagination on a piece of paper (in reality, it was probably more like thousands of pieces of paper). I did have help from an awesome builder and a drafting firm in Springfield, plus some input from my wonderful husband and kids, but the design and layout was all mine.

I grew up in Oklahoma, with a father who was a Realtor and builder/developer. I worked in his office nearly every summer from age 14 to college graduation. Therefore, I have always been interested in all things real estate and the "American Dream" of home ownership.

My dad also remodeled all three of our family homes over the years to suit our family's specific needs. He was always excited when he could pull off something to "just fit" in an available space, or make unique changes that customized the house to fit our family's needs.

My father's problem-solving skills and creativity must have rubbed off on me, because I have also been involved in remodeling or upgrading all four of the houses I have owned in my lifetime, before building this one, my dream home. I didn't even realize that fact until looking back on all my previous experiences while writing this book! I guess I have never been satisfied with any house just the way it was.

I have enjoyed sketching out different versions of my "dream home" since I was in junior high school. I think I have always had some version of what I thought was the perfect floor plan floating around in my head, but I really got into it when we bought the lake lot.

To those who say, "Why not just hire an architect? That's what they do." My advice is to go for it. They will help you design your home, see the project through to completion, and save you lots of time and trouble. I also highly recommend an architect if you are not very knowledgeable about the subject of real estate and design. Hiring an architect is a wonderful idea if you can afford it.

But if you are like me, you would rather design your own home. That's why you are reading this book, right? And not everyone can afford an architect. Even if you do decide to go with an architect, you still need some idea of what you want in the house and its layout. The architect will have lots of questions for you about what you want, so that they can design it specifically for you. They will also want some input from you on your style and tastes. The more of this kind of decisions you can make and agree on ahead of time, the better. Also, there are good architects and not-so-good ones, and some are easier to work with than others. Therefore, educating yourself is a good thing.

If you are going to use an architect and/or a designer, you might want to visit with them briefly before you begin planning. You can usually have a first consultation, with little or no charge, just to get an idea of what you are getting yourself into. You can also visit with several firms to find the one you feel you can work with best.

My purpose in writing this book is twofold. One, to share what I learned (including my mistakes) over the past 25 years. Two, to help pay off the mortgage on said dream home with whatever meager proceeds I may make from this book in the process. Building plans will also be available for purchase, for those who would rather use my plans than create their own (see Chapter 16).

Choosing a floor plan (from the millions already out there in books and magazines), coming up with your own design, or narrowing down the choices with an architect, is not as easy as it sounds. It is a very complex process. There are just too many choices and infinite possibilities. And you want to make sure that you are happy with the finished product, as there are no "do-overs" here. I just hope this book doesn't turn you into one of those customers who drives the architect or builder crazy because you know too much (or not quite enough)!

One way to narrow down the choices or begin laying out your dream home is by looking at many buildings and houses that are already built. I am a tactile-kinesthetic learner, which means that I want to touch, feel and move around in what I am learning about, not just hear it or see it on paper. Therefore, for me it is easier to decide on a layout by actually touring/walking through an existing room or building, and that way you don't have to "picture" what it would look like. You can see it, touch it, stand in it, measure it and actually look around.

3

Anyone who has house-hunted with a Realtor (or on their own), or watched "House Hunters" on HGTV, knows that no house is perfect. Unless you have all the money in the world, the one you buy is just the one in your price range that has the most things on your "want list." You can avoid this if you design your own house, right? Wrong!

I have known many people who have custom built a house and were then disappointed in how it turned out. Mostly, they've said it was smaller than what they had pictured. Or they said, "if only our house had...," "looking back, I wish we had...," or "I didn't even think about..." So I was determined that this would not happen to me.

For more than 25 years, literally, I measured living rooms, kitchens, motel rooms, cabins, friends' houses, decks, cabinets, countertops, garages, furniture, etc. I had to get an idea what ten feet or twenty-five feet really looked like in real life, and what that measurement would hold in the way of furniture, people and traffic. I also wanted the best layout and the most efficient use of space possible.

I have never seen any published floor plan that I liked just the way it was. I may have liked one thing about this one, or thought that one had a good idea in a few rooms, but none were ever just right all the way through. That's why it never occurred to me NOT to design my own floor plan! Therefore, I am sharing what I learned throughout the whole process in hopes of preventing someone from having regrets after it is too late. When building your dream home, all of your decisions are so permanent, so plan ahead.

I've obviously learned a lot about structure and design over the decades since Junior High School. My original college major was interior design, so I got enough drafting and design education to be able to draw floor plans with good traffic patterns and efficient spaces. I also learned to draw all the little symbols like doorways and windows before I changed my major to education.

That's right. I am not an architect, nor am I an engineer. I just happen to be a regular person who has always been intrigued with houses and studying/drawing various floor plan ideas. Perhaps I should have been an architect instead of a teacher, but I definitely found my "calling" in education, so wouldn't change a thing. I am now a retired speech/language pathologist and special education teacher. I taught full time for 30 years and raised three children. So I was by no means working at these floor plans more than sporadically, until the last few years as we got nearer to retirement age.

Designing floor plans has always been just a "hobby" until I had the chance to actually build one. I will be eternally grateful to my husband for letting me really do it. Three times, actually! My first opportunity to build one of my designs was in 1998, when we added on to our family home in Oklahoma. That one only took me 8 years! Seriously, designing that addition didn't take that long. Most of that time was spent convincing my husband that it was a good idea to add on to the house. But once it was finished, we were really pleased with how that addition turned out and how functional it was.

Several years later, we gutted our kitchen in that same house and built a new one, which I absolutely loved. So with those two successful experiences under my belt, I was even more excited about designing our lake house for the future. Many of my best ideas from those projects were incorporated into the lake house designs as well.

Over the years, I must have had hundreds, maybe even thousands, of starts on my dream floor plan. But whenever I saw a house or building feature that I liked, or thought of a cool idea, I would go "back to the drawing board", literally. I ended up with boxes full of floor plan books, decorating magazines, architectural books, and designs I had drawn at different times and stages of our lives.

Our hobbies and interests also changed during those 25 years of drawing floor plans. When we were younger, my husband was really into photography. My plans then always included a dark room for him to develop his own film and print his own pictures. He was also into woodworking, so early plans also included a separate workshop off the garage. With the advent of personal computers and digital cameras, the darkroom need obviously dissolved. The workshop also dwindled to only a small area in the front part of the garage, which is what we have now. The plans we ended up with for the lake house are completely different from the house I would have built 20 or 30 years ago.

I am not recommending that you take 25 years to plan your dream home, just giving reasons why you need to take your time and do a lot of thinking before you begin. There is no way to predict what science and technology may come up with, let alone what lifestyle changes may occur in your life. But it is a good idea to at least consider how things might change in your future (having kids or more kids; the kids getting bigger and needing more space; or children growing up and leaving home, thereby needing less space; extended family moving in to be cared for as they age; or your own changing needs in health and mobility as you age, to name a few). If you take your time planning before you start, you will be more assured of ending up with what you need and want down the road.

For most people, moving is a stressful and traumatic experience, so you don't want to do it any more often than necessary. The more thought and consideration you put into your house plans, and the more adaptable your layout can be, the longer your dream home will suit your needs. That way you can update your house as your needs change without having to move and start over. And planning ample storage space so everything has a place will also help your dream home STAY your dream home for longer.

We all accumulate too much "stuff" over time, which makes us think we need a bigger house. But often times, just organizing your "stuff" and getting rid of the excess will make your current home livable for longer. You can never have too much storage! Remember that when you are designing your spaces.

I mentioned above that I had some drafting experience in college, but I obviously did NOT get the training I needed to undertake this project in real life. It was easy to draw whatever I wanted when it was all a pipe dream. And free. But when it became a reality to actually build what I had designed, it really opened my eyes about what I did NOT know! I also made several costly mistakes, which I mention at other places throughout the book. I have told many people that if I had the information from this book before I started, I could have saved up to a third of my actual building costs. I obviously learned a lot in the process, and I hope that my experiences and what I learned will help you design the best dream home possible for your needs.

And don't worry. No matter what you draw or sketch, it will be structurally sound because you will consult people who actually know what they are doing before you turn a shovel. I took my designs to an architectural/drafting firm to review and draw my designs in "blueprint"/building plan form so my builder and his crew could build it to my exact spec's. I only paid a small percentage for this compared to what it would have cost to have an architect design the whole thing. But I could not and would not have done it without the drafting firm putting my dreams into a form others could work from. And if there are any mistakes in your floor plans that won't work as you have designed them, an architect or an experienced architectural draftsman can correct them for you. They can also sometimes even give you ideas you hadn't thought of to make your plans even better.

I don't know how I finally came up with a final floor plan that I thought was good enough to actually build, but somehow I managed to narrow down the choices and come up with a "keeper". The finished product just incorporated all the good ideas I had come up with over the years, and other people's ideas I liked, and combined them all into this one "perfect" plan. There's only one problem with my "perfect" floor plan. That is, it is MY perfect plan, not yours. Therefore, I would like to share the process with you about how I came up with MY perfect layout/design. That way, you can come up with your OWN perfect plan! There is no one perfect floor plan for everybody, or all homes would be alike!

One more thing before I begin. Building a house from the ground up is very time consuming, and you aren't even doing the actual work! Just be aware that the more prepared you are before beginning, the smoother the process will go and the less stressful it will be. It is an awesome project to undertake, but you will probably have an actual life, also (job, kids, family, etc.) while you are building. Therefore, you need to make it as easy on yourself and your family as possible by doing your "homework" ahead of time.

There are hundreds of choices that need to be made while you are building, and many of them may need to be made in a fairly short period of time. Building materials, stone/brick/siding, roofing, tile/hardwood/carpet, countertops, plumbing, appliances, paint color, trim, décor, etc., all need to be picked out at some point in the process. If you have made the majority of these selections prior to actually breaking ground, it will help streamline your project considerably. But when your builder is ready for you to pick out certain products, be sure to go back to your source or store to verify that what you originally settled on is still what you want. Double-checking with your supplier also reduces the possibility of errors in ordering!

It is imperative that you do not make the builder or construction crew wait on you to make up your mind on materials and choices. This costs them (and you) time, money, and scheduling delays like a domino effect, for both your building project and others already on the schedule. Indecision on your part can cause a major set-back in your progress, so I suggest you do lots of planning ahead. The more decisions you can make on what you want, before you start building, the better.

We were retired and living in a little 900 square foot cabin up the hill from the lot while we were building. That way, I could devote full time to watching our dream house take shape. I was also available at a moment's notice to answer questions or make choices about what I wanted here or there. That was really helpful to us and the builder. I would often just jump in the golf cart and run down the hill to watch the guys work. It was really fascinating to watch every square inch as it went up. I think it made the crews a little nervous sometimes, for me to just sit there and stare at them, but it was fun for me!

I realize that ours was the best case scenario, and most people would not have the luxury to just drop everything and run down to the building site whenever asked. But I would hope that you would be in a position to at least check on the progress regularly. It is nice to be able to conveniently participate in the process without adding too much stress to your lives!

CHAPTER TWO

LAYOUT AND DESIGN

I may be getting the cart before the horse, talking about the layout and design of your home before discussing the location. However, if you don't already have your lot or site picked out, the layout you choose may influence your decisions on what topography (ground slope, etc.) you will need in order to build what you want. If you already have your lot, it may dictate what layout you go with. The next two chapters after this one deal with size and location so you can consider all three before you begin.

The main thrust of this chapter is two-fold: (1) to establish the general shape and appearance of what you want, and (2) to give you general design information to incorporate into whatever layout you come up with. The more information you have on designing your dream home, the more likely you are to end up with a house that meets your specific needs and tastes. Hopefully, much of what I learned will shorten your design process and increase the chances that you will love the end result of your efforts.

I am a very detail-oriented person, with probably a little OCD mixed in, so I hope I don't overwhelm you with too much information and attention to detail. Some of it you may need, some you may not; some you may already know, and some may be totally foreign concepts to you. I wanted to write this book so that even the most inexperienced novice could pick it up and benefit from it. But I don't mean to insult anyone's intelligence, either. For all readers, I have tried to provide as complete an overview as possible of things to consider when planning your dream home.

I will give more details on specific rooms and features in later chapters, but wanted to give you some general layout considerations before you get started. As stated in my introduction, I really did spend 25 years playing with various options and layouts before finally coming up with our "dream" floor plan. Hopefully, you won't spend more than a few weeks or months on this process, but I wouldn't take any of my experiences back. I loved every minute of it, and would recommend it to anyone who needed to do it a step at a time like we did. Sometimes, like planning a vacation, the preparation is nearly as much fun as the actual trip! Now let's get started.

Get organized. As a first step, I would suggest you find some type of notebook or record-keeping system, and just start jotting down all your ideas. Be sure to LABEL your container or whatever you decide to use. I am giving this advice because, over the years, I had several piles, files, and boxes of separate notes, ideas, and drawings scattered around, and it was difficult to round them all up when I was finally ready to start drawing my actual building plans.

When you are writing down your ideas, of course you will want to include features that you want. But also include, specifically, features that you DON'T want. For instance, you may want walk-out attic storage but not a split-level floor plan. I didn't want any stairs in my floor plan due to our age.

I was particularly picky about our building location. One thing that was important to me was not being too near a creek or river bottom that might flash flood and destroy our home. We lived through a 200 year flood once, and I vowed never again. Our house didn't flood, but we were in constant fear as the water rose on three sides of our house. And I saw what it did to other houses that weren't so lucky.

Another thing that I always look at is the areas' streets and driveway slopes, in case of snow and ice in the winter. I personally would also avoid building on a steep slope or bluff for fear of mud slides. We live in the national forest, so I worry about wildfires. But I wouldn't have it any other way since I love trees. Being from Oklahoma originally, I would avoid a hill top or open plain so I didn't become tornado bait. The East or North side of a hill would then be my choice.

Whatever features and concerns are important to you, write them down. If you do use an architect, they can take all of these into consideration as they are designing for you. And if you don't have your lot yet, you can buy according to your "want list" as well as area preferences and concerns.

You have your own ideas, so start documenting them. You don't have to agree on anything at this point, just write down whatever comes to mind. This list will stand you in good stead when you (or your architect) start drawing. And some people have difficulty making up their minds quickly, especially when under pressure, so take your time (ahead of time) to feel more confident in your choices. Remember, you don't want your builder and crew waiting on you to make up your mind after you have already started building!

Don't forget, when buying a house already on the market, you probably won't get all the features you want. But when custom designing your dream home, you can get ALL your "must-haves", if you can remember (and afford) them all! But I guarantee, you will not remember everything you have thought of if you don't write them down. You don't want to forget a cool feature that you later regret not adding space for.

When you start drawing floor plans, be sure to hang on to the working pages you like before you make changes to it – you may want to come back to an idea in that one later and won't be able to remember how you laid out a particular feature. By all means, throw away the ones you don't like! Just hang on to ideas you come up with that you do like, even if you decide to change them. I did all mine the old fashioned way, on graph paper, so threw away ones that didn't work but hung onto ones I liked until I was positive I wouldn't be using them. Most people now will do their designing online. There are many good computer drafting programs out there.

If you use an architect, they will also need to know the features you want included in the design. The more details you can give them about what you want, the easier it will be for them to design something you will absolutely love. Going "back to the drawing board" may add to the total expense if you later change your mind and want to make alterations to the building plans. The more you know before you start, the less likely you will want to make costly changes later on. Also, if you keep track of all your ideas and "want list" during the planning stages, you can be sure they get included in the final design and added correctly when you actually break ground.

General Layout and roof line. The least expensive design for building a house is a simple square or rectangle with a single, straight roof line. Every corner you turn adds to the total building costs. However, if you are custom-designing your own home, you will probably want something a little more appealing than a simple rectangle. But you can do amazing things with just a little tweaking to that basic shape. Just remember, the more turns or corners you add to the outside walls, and the more changes in roof line from a simple rectangle, the more expensive it will be to build.

The following illustration shows some roof line options for your dream house, but of course you can design it with any shape you can dream up! Just remember, the more complex the shape, the more expensive it will be to build, regardless of the size.

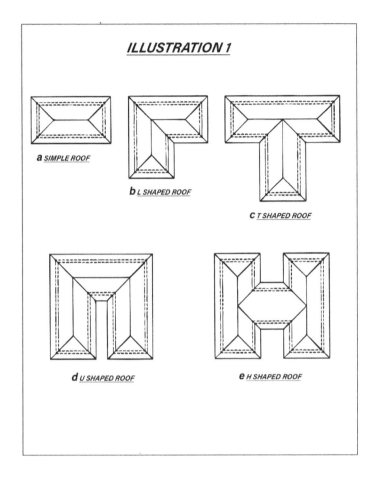

You could take your basic rectangle and add a single covered front porch, and/or add a deck out back without changing your roof line, thereby adding some curb appeal without much added expense. I started with a large rectangle and added pretty simple parts to it, starting with an "L" on one end and vaulted ceilings in the middle. Many newer homes seem to have lots of roof and wall changes, gables, turrets, turns and twists, all of which add to the building cost by a substantial amount. Some newer homes are gorgeous with all those details, but on others I just see a waste of money. If that's the style you like, be prepared to pay for it. That's why you want to choose your own design. Everybody's tastes are different, as are their budgets.

In the following illustration, you can see how much difference in curb appeal the covered front porch adds to a simple rectangle. Drawing "c" is an exaggerated example of a more complex design, showing all the angles and extra turns that can increase construction costs ridiculously. Landscaping can also dramatically affect the curb appeal of a pretty simple house.

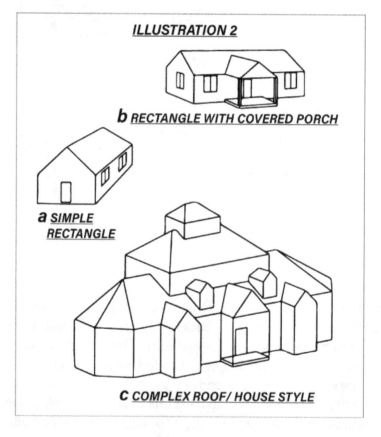

ILLUSTRATION 2

b RECTANGLE WITH COVERED PORCH

a SIMPLE RECTANGLE

C COMPLEX ROOF/ HOUSE STYLE

If your roof line stays simple, you can always add porches or decks under roof without changing the foundation or roof much, thus adding curb appeal without adding much expense. Consider the "H" shaped house in illustration 1 e. If you extended the roof and foundation across the "H" and put a porch under roof in front and back, it would make the actual roof and foundation lines in a simple square or rectangle shape. This would still give you the "H" configuration inside, but the outside lines would be a little less expensive to construct.

I suggest, as you start "playing" with your design layout, that you just sketch a rectangle and start deciding where your different rooms could be. If you don't have enough room for everything you want, you can always enlarge the rectangle or add a turn or "wing" somewhere, or design it with a basement and/or second story. Multiple stories are also cheaper than single stories for the same total square footage. Remember, it doesn't cost anything to draw pictures! And there is no right or wrong at this stage. You don't even need to worry too much about drawing to scale at first, just to sketch layout ideas. Often times, an idea would come to me as I sketched, or I would get a cool idea for something that would just "fit" in a leftover corner or between two rooms.

To get an idea of how much space or length to allow for certain features, walls, or room sizes, measure what you currently have. Whether you own or rent your current living quarters, you can start with what you have. Measure the things you like, and write down or sketch (with the dimensions) how you would change or improve it if you could. For instance, if your current kitchen island is 4 feet long and you wish it were 5 feet, then design your "dream" kitchen island to be 5 or 6 feet long, to be sure it will turn out long enough to fit your needs. If you like certain features of your parents' or a friend's home, ask if you can measure them. Then write down the idea and sketch out measurements, taking a picture if you like. If you see something in a showroom that you think is a keeper, measure it and then sketch the layout. WRITE IT DOWN!

Style. You need to figure out what your style is before going too far. There are several ways to accomplish this. You know what you like when driving around town. Start there and maybe take

17

pictures of your favorites. Then you could start looking at house pictures online or in books and magazines. You will need to look at the outside of many houses as well as inside features to get a feel for your design tastes. Then you will probably want to visit lots of stores and showrooms.

As with drawing pictures, it doesn't cost anything to look at different products and prices. But again, write down or take pictures of the things you like! If you don't mind getting "junk mail" from Realtors, you could also visit open houses when they are advertised. This doesn't cost any money, and you can get lots of ideas touring actual homes that are for sale.

One of my favorite activities when I was younger was to drive around neighborhoods and look at houses that are already built. If you find one that you particularly like, it is easy enough to take a picture with your cell phone. Be aware, though, that if you are driving very slowly through a neighborhood and stop more than momentarily to take pictures, you may look suspicious to others and someone may call the police on you!

Do you want a show place, or a practical home that just suits your needs? Or are you interested in exploring the "tiny home" concept? I would think most people would want some of each – a beautiful AND practical design. If you really want the "wow" factor, I would suggest you consult an architect. But I knew what I wanted, and what I wanted it to look like, from looking at houses and designs all my life.

The following illustration shows actual photographs of my finished "dream home".

My personal tastes run more to the eclectic, and "rustic elegance" decor, so lots of wood and stone fits my style. But one of my sons likes clean modern lines and is more of a minimalist. He would probably prefer a design with lots of metal and glass. Some people like the country look while others may prefer Victorian, antique, traditional, craftsman, contemporary, or whatever. And there are no rules today in what you choose. Many people now combine antique with modern elements in the same room and they can look really good together. You don't even have to match colors or patterns any more, though I still prefer to do that in my own spaces to some degree.

You don't have to have a degree in interior design to know what you like. You just have to look around enough to know what suits you. However, if you have no experience in this area, I would at least listen to the sales people as you are picking things out, because they may have more experience in what looks good together. It's always nice to have a second opinion. If you know you have NO talent in this area, please consult a decorator, designer, and/or architect. I would hate for you to end up with something that is really not appealing.

Luckily, my husband and I had a fairly easy time picking out materials and fixtures because we have similar tastes. If you are single, go for it. But if you and your spouse/partner have very different tastes, be prepared that it will take longer to choose the features that appeal to both of you. Just keep looking until you find those things that you BOTH like. It CAN be done!

Space and efficiency. Designing efficiency into your spaces is key to not only saving money as you build, but also to increasing the convenience factor in your daily life after you move in. From carting laundry all over the house, to waiting too long for hot water in the shower, you want to consider efficiency when designing your spaces. This section deals with several factors that may affect cost, convenience and efficiency.

My design has three main parts: (1) the public areas in the center (living room, dining room, and kitchen); (2) the bedroom "wing" on one side; and (3) the garage/office on the other side. Most homes have two main parts: public and private. There is no rule saying how you have to organize your layout. But there are considerations in cost and efficiency that may affect your decisions.

Obviously, you want your dining space convenient to the kitchen, and every bedroom to have easy access to a bathroom. But there are numerous other factors to consider as well. Location of rooms, appliances and furniture in relation to each other, plumbing, traffic, and storage are all parts of the whole. Square footage is definitely not the only consideration when planning your spaces.

For layout ideas, think of your daily routine when you are at home. You want the location of your rooms, in relation to each other, to be efficient and convenient for the activities you enjoy daily. You might want to cluster rooms together that you use most often. Or you might come up with a storage idea perfectly placed for a particular activity you perform frequently. These are the specific kinds of things that make your plans "custom" to your specific needs.

I put my husband's "man cave" (in this case, his office) just inside the house from the garage. That way it is convenient to the rest of the house, or secluded if the door is closed. I also built myself a sewing room ("woman cave" – hey, why not?) beside the laundry room. When I sew, I need easy access to the iron (which is in the laundry room), so it made sense to put my sewing room next to the laundry room. Also, since I do both the sewing and laundry in our household, the two rooms kind of combine as "my spaces" and are also near the master bedroom. My husband's "man cave" is on the opposite side of the house, which gives us each our own space. Both the office for him and the sewing room for me have closets, so they can double as extra bedrooms if needed. The "man cave" could also be used as a "mother-in-law" bedroom instead, if that is a feature you would need.

Even your garage configuration, size and shape can be customized to your specific needs. The restrictive covenants in our area limited our garage size to no more than two cars, but I wanted ample storage and workshop space included. So I made each garage door 9 feet wide instead of 8, with extra space between the doors and on both sides. I also allowed a longer depth to allow workshop space in the front of the garage.

I knew one woman who designed a laundry/craft room for herself that was nearly the size of a two-car garage! She also had a huge square "island" taking up much of the middle of the room for storage and workspace. Obviously, most of us don't have that kind of money, but it was an awesome idea and very well designed. I was jealous.

While planning your design, remember to consider bathrooms and laundry in your layout. I have devoted an entire chapter to bathrooms and laundry later, but these need to be considered early on in your planning for space and efficiency purposes. For example, how long will it take for hot water to get from where you put the water heater to each location needing the hot water (bathrooms, kitchen, laundry room). You might want to consider two smaller water heaters over one large one, or the newer "on-demand" water heaters.

Another thing you need to consider is that it is cheaper to put plumbing areas near each other. Plumbing and pipes that have to go all the way across your house to a lone bathroom will cost more to build than if you run them to only one or two areas of your home. If you cluster the rooms needing water, you could save quite a bit in construction costs. For example, try putting a bathroom butting up to the kitchen wall, or the laundry room next to a bathroom. The more spread out your plumbing fixtures are, the more expensive it will be to build. Please see Chapter 5 for more information on plumbing.

Don't forget that your clothes dryer needs to be either on or next to an outside wall to vent the warm moist air to the outside. You can't put the laundry room in the center of the house because there would be no way to vent the dryer efficiently. But you can put it between bedrooms as long as it is on an outside wall. And you really should try to run all pipes on inside walls instead of outside walls to help protect them from cold weather.

Another consideration in space planning is passageways for getting from room to room. I have a personal bias against hallways, as I feel they are a waste of square footage. They may be a necessary way to get from point A to Point B in larger homes, schools or commercial buildings that have lots of rooms needing to be accessed. But to me, short hallways or alcoves are a more efficient use of space in most homes. An alcove can allow access to 2 or 3 rooms at a time using a minimal amount of floor space. On the other hand, a hallway leading to all bedrooms and bathrooms does separate the public and private areas better, in terms of noise and privacy. So you decide which is better for your design.

Illustration 4, below, shows the difference between a hallway and an alcove in accessing two bedrooms and a bathroom. Both pictures are the same square footage. Notice the increased bedroom square footage when you use an alcove instead of a hallway.

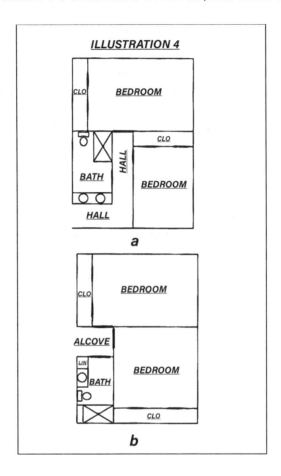

I guess it depends on the amount of separation you desire. Since we were retired and it was supposed to be just the two of us living here most of the time, we didn't think we needed that much separation or privacy. But now that two of our adult children have temporarily moved back in with us, sometimes I wish I had designed it a little differently.

Entry. Do you want a designated entry area at the front door? Do you want people to enter directly into your formal living room? Dining room? Kitchen? The front door/main entry location was one of the first things I planned, from an outside (front of the house) perspective. Then I went from there to "build" the rest of the house. I also wanted the front door to be only a short walk from where I parked my car, or guests parked theirs, for easy access into the house. Your front door/entry area is one of the most important parts of your outside curb appeal, and it needs to be easily recognized from outside so guests can easily find your front door. I know this sounds obvious, but I've seen some houses where it was not so easy to figure out where the front door was, which makes the whole house feel less welcoming.

Normally, guests to your home would enter from the front door into a designated area near the living room. This area should ideally have a coat closet nearby and/or some kind of storage for outer wear, umbrellas, etc. I would also tile this area instead of carpeting or hardwood, so it could stand up to the dirt and moisture coming in.

If you want a designated entry "hall", be sure to make it wide and long enough to accommodate the number of people coming and going. For instance, there may be several guests entering at one time, and there needs to be room for them to pass you (the host/hostess) as you invite them in. There may also be a "log jam" as people take off their coats, bring in packages, maneuver a stroller, etc., so plan your space accordingly.

Wherever guests will enter, don't forget that the entry will be their first impression of your entire home. The entry area should be well lit so that your home does not appear dark and dreary. You may want to consider what they will see first when you open the front door. You may also want to be able to see from the inside who is at the door for security purposes, so plan your entry accordingly.

You and your family, when arriving home daily, may enter from a different location than guests. Will you be entering through the front door? Garage or carport? Side or back door? Whatever suits your lifestyle, make sure your entry areas are large enough to accommodate your needs and habits. If you and your family members enter from the back door, for instance, this area should also accommodate outer wear, wet boots, etc. I also have hooks for coats and keys at each entrance in our house.

Your family's entrance, whether it be the front door or another area, will usually be where you put down your purse, keys, mail, etc., as you enter. If this is your pattern, you must have a table or cabinet handy for this purpose. An end table with a decorative basket on it may suffice, or you may want a larger cabinet with drawers. If you carry your mail and other things on into the kitchen or living area, there should still be a designated space for such items in whatever room you choose. If you do not plan for this, the clutter will end up on your kitchen or dining room table, the island/bar, or some other catch-all surface.

Public/living areas. Your first decisions on layout should center around the more public areas in your home such as the main entry, living and dining area(s), kitchen and garage. Think about your daily routine, and plan your design accordingly. Most house plans have the kitchen adjacent to the garage so that you can easily enter the kitchen from the garage with your groceries. If you will not be using your garage all the time and will be entering through the front door, or if your floor plan does not have a garage, I strongly suggest that you have a covered front porch so entry is easier and safer in inclement weather.

I also suggest that the kitchen be easily accessible from your entry or garage so you don't have as far to go with your groceries before setting them down. I picture the phone ringing as I come in the door with an armload of groceries. How long does it take me to set stuff down and answer the phone? Even if you don't have a land line, you still have to set your bundles down before you can answer your cell phone or whatever.

Some houses have the garage under the house. This means that every time you come home, you will be carrying everything from the car up the stairs to the house. The garage in the basement may be an efficient use of space, but to me it is not very practical. Again, it is a matter of opinion and your needs. Maybe I am just too old to think about hauling all that stuff up the stairs every day! Maybe if you had a lift or an elevator to the main floor, I would think about it differently. Of course, I wouldn't have a clue how expensive that would be. Again, whatever design works best for you and your budget is great! If you come up with some cool and unique ideas, it can really personalize your space. After all, this is about customizing your "dream home," right?

You obviously need to plan your living space(s) efficiently, as well. Do you need a formal dining room? Eating space in the kitchen? Family room off an open kitchen? Game room? Pool table? Large dining table to seat an extended family? Home theater? Wet bar? You will also want to plan convenient access to all these spaces from one to another. "Crowd control" and traffic flow may also be a factor if you do a lot of entertaining.

When designing your living/family areas, be sure and plan your conversation groupings and t.v. watching areas carefully. With recliners, sectional sofas, reclining or chaise sofas, and a myriad of chairs to choose from, there are endless ways to arrange your living areas. You want to make sure that your t.v. is placed for comfortable viewing for a number of people or angles, and that there is adequate comfortable seating (appropriate for however many in your household/family will be watching together). You also want to make sure that there are plenty of outlets to plug things in and hook up cables so you can arrange the room the way you want. You might want cable hook-ups on more than one wall in any given room, and at least one electrical outlet on each wall. Your builder will ask you about placing these, so give it some thought.

When the t.v. is not on, you will want to have the seating arranged for comfortable conversation or other leisure activities in your living area(s). Remember that a social conversation is easier when facing the other person (sitting across from them) rather than when sitting right beside them (as in side-by-side on a couch). So you really do need more than just a sofa or couch, even if it just means adding one side chair. And don't forget to allow enough space for end tables, coffee tables, etc.

You must design your spaces to be large enough to accommodate whatever you want to put in them, and still be able to get around the room. Allowing space for traffic through a room is critical. And every door, air vent, window, etc., may affect how things fit in a room or how you would arrange your furniture. If you don't consider these factors ahead of time, you may be disappointed with your finished design, as it will not work as well for your needs as it could have.

My husband teased me that I was designing an entire room around a $20 sofa. Duh! That is the whole crux of a custom design! You have to decide what furniture you want to put in a room and then make sure the dimensions that you draw for that room will hold the furniture you want to put there. Of course, I did not design a room around a $20 sofa, but I did make sure an 8 foot sofa would fit on a particular wall, and that I had room for my piano in the living room that did not interfere with the conversation area. I also made sure that, with end tables on either side of the sofa, the living room was going to be wide enough for people to be able to get around and between the pieces of furniture easily to sit down.

I would also consider the amount of open floor space within each room, where there is no furniture placed. The more of this space that there is in a room, the more versatile the room is. Think of the whole family sitting around together watching t.v. Is there room on the floor for a baby's play pen without blocking the t.v.? Or a group of kids playing a board game on the floor? Think of your current and future lifestyle and needs when designing your spaces. You will be glad you did!

I think it is imperative to consider traffic through the living room when designing your layout. You don't want to bump into furniture, cross in front of someone watching t.v. (or having a conversation), or find it difficult to walk through a room that has too much furniture in it. Traffic is an important part of the overall design of every room and I discuss this concept in the next section.

Traffic. The next step in designing your overall layout is traffic flow. The path that people take when walking around from one place to another through the inside of your house can be viewed as "traffic". You must picture where people will go and how they will get there during their daily routines, as well as party functions or a crowd, around the house. Start at the front door and picture yourself going into a bedroom or bathroom. Or start in the garage and picture yourself bringing groceries in. How would you get from the baby's room to the front door? Or the laundry room to the bedrooms to put laundry away?

The location of doorways will determine to a great extent how people will travel through a room, from one doorway to another. This will also have a great impact on your furniture arrangement and traffic. You must know that people can easily enter, cross, and leave every room with a minimum of interference from furniture placement. You also want a minimum of disruption to whatever activities are going on in the room when they pass through. You also have to know that the furniture you want to put in a room will fit, and still leave ample room to move around in the room. You should allow a minimum of 3 feet of width as a passageway between pieces of furniture for people to easily pass through an area, allowing for them to maybe also be carrying a bundle, baby, laundry basket, groceries, etc.

Poor traffic planning is one of my pet peeves. Our last family house had a family room with the two doors diagonally across the room from each other. Very poor design! It was very difficult to arrange furniture in that room, and I was constantly re-arranging the furniture to come up with a better plan. If the two doors are directly across the room from each other, or the plan is very open, then the traffic flow is much more efficient, as is the possibility of good furniture placement. This cannot always be done, but should at least be considered for the majority of your rooms.

I personally don't like having traffic through the middle of my furniture grouping or t.v. watching. So I designed our current family room with no "through" traffic. A sofa acts as the divider between the family room and the kitchen. So I left enough room for all traffic to flow behind the sofa rather than through the family room. We had to measure carefully to make sure we allowed enough room for the bar stools AND people walking through the area, but it works great. We are very pleased with the end result, but it did take a lot of planning. I also extended the kitchen tile to end just behind the sofa, which saves the carpet in the family room from all that traffic, soil and wear.

The following illustration shows our kitchen/family room layout. Notice the space between the kitchen bar and the back of the sofa as a traffic area. It works fabulously.

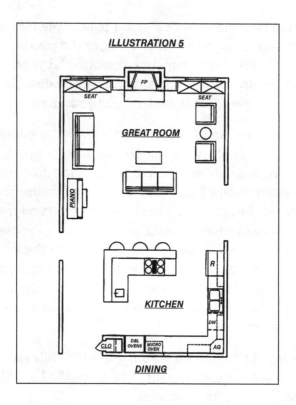

You also want to avoid "choke points" in the entry and hallways, and within each room. Choke points are where two people cannot pass each other without one having to step out of the way, or where one person's presence blocks everyone else's movement through an area. Preventing these blockages in traffic takes quite a bit of planning.

Traffic planning is an area where an architect could save you lots of time and brain power. This is what architects do. They don't just design pretty buildings. They take a myriad of factors into account when designing a space. This is another reason to run your plans through a drafting/architectural firm before breaking ground, so you know that a professional has approved your design. You are still the designer in this case, but they have the experience and expertise to help you "tweak" your layout so that it is the best it can be. In this case, you are paying the professional for his or her expertise on a consulting basis, since you are acting as the architect of your own home, and the cost should be much less by spending your own "man-hours" rather than the architect's expensive labor.

Private areas/bedrooms. After you get your priorities decided for the more public areas of your home, you need to decide where to put your other rooms. Will you have a designated office space? How many bedrooms and bathrooms do you need? What about storage and closets? Future chapters will address many of these issues, but I wanted to be sure you gave this a good amount of thought early on in the planning stages.

If you want a separate office, do you want it near the entry for clients, or at the back of the house for quiet and privacy? Or will you have an office space built into the kitchen? If your lap top or tablet is to be in the kitchen, for example, be sure to allow enough space for convenient use without interfering with the daily functions of the kitchen. It would be difficult to try and work in an area that didn't have adequate desk space without competing with space for cooking, dirty dishes, or groceries on the counter.

If you need special rooms for specific purposes, there may be unique features needed. If you want a music room, for example, you need to consider that you don't put a piano on an outside wall (due to temperature and moisture changes, noise, etc.). A music room may also need to be separated from other parts of the house due to noise. For an art "studio", you also need to consider the sources of natural sunlight entering that room and from what direction(s). How many windows? Skylights? It may make a difference which side of the house to put a certain room on, depending on your needs. My covered deck is on the East side of the house so it is not as hot in the afternoons. Just don't forget to plan these types of details for your lifestyle.

Do you want your bedrooms to all be near each other, or would you rather they be more separated for privacy? Also remember the need for separation from the living areas for both noise control and privacy. And separation for sound needs to be addressed between bedrooms if you have a new baby or several children who may wake each other up at night or nap time. There is also such a thing as sound separation and insulation that you may want to put in certain walls, floors, or ceilings. You may want the master bedroom to be near small children or separated from kids' or guest rooms for privacy.

Our kids were all adults when we built this house, so privacy was more important than being near the kids' or guest rooms. I put closets between all my bedrooms so that the sound problems from one to another would be minimized. I put a bathroom and the laundry room between the kid and adult spaces in our house. Between closets, bathrooms, halls and the laundry room, you can arrange the rooms so that there are few, if any, shared walls. And if you design a two-story house (or more), remember that noise from upstairs kids' rooms can be very irritating if placed over a downstairs bedroom. And the laundry room should never go in the basement or garage! Most of the laundry generated will go to the bedrooms, so I would put it near or between the majority of the sleeping areas.

What is the most effective placement for your bathrooms? Be sure to have at least one full bath in the vicinity of the bedrooms, and plan a separate "en suite" bathroom for the master bedroom. Even if you don't think you need that feature, the resale value of your house will be reduced if you do not have an en suite bathroom for the master bedroom. Most newer houses also have double sinks for the master bathroom, as well as a separate tub AND shower.

A half bath off the living area is also a necessity as far as I am concerned, so guests don't have to see your cluttered bedrooms on their way to the bathroom. You don't want the half bath to open right off the kitchen or living room, but you can place it right around a corner somewhere in the vicinity of where you would do the most entertaining. There should also be at least a half bath on each floor, if you have a basement or second story. A mud room off the back yard is also a nice feature, if that is something you would use.

In my opinion, every house should have at least 2 ½ bathrooms, but any more than that is what I would consider to be a luxury. And since bathrooms and kitchens are the most expensive per square foot to put in, you should plan accordingly to prevent excessive costs. Please see my chapters on the kitchen and bathrooms for more details.

Cautions. I mentioned in my introduction that I made several costly mistakes in the process of building my dream home. In most cases, the design was ok, but the fixtures and other purchases could have been better planned, especially my lighting and electrical choices. I may have spent 25 years on the design, but sometimes only hours on some of the surfaces and fixtures, so hadn't thought all of that through nearly as much as the layout. I also hadn't had as much experience with that part of the process. I will discuss this more in later chapters.

Your builder, designer and/or architect can help you with estimating costs of any features you feel are "must-haves". They may even give you an "allowance" for many of your choices. For instance, they may give you a budget for a certain cost per square foot to stay within when choosing flooring (carpet, tile, hardwood), and if you go over that, you realize that your total cost will go up or you have to cut costs elsewhere. But you may have to ask them how much added features or fixtures will increase the total cost estimate. I do wish I had gone a little more practical in some of my choices and less "wow" factor, because we would have saved a lot of money. But there are also many instances where I am very happy that I went with the higher quality/cost features.

Impulse changes or upgrades as you are building can also really put you over budget. That's why you need to make as many decisions up front as possible so there are fewer surprises along the way. Again, it is all a matter of individual taste and budget.

If you use an architect, the builder/contractor will usually report directly to him or her, and you will mostly deal with the architect. If you do not have an architect, you will be dealing with the builder/contractor directly. Depending on your builder, most can do whatever you want, as long as you have building plans for them to follow. When you submit your floor plans to the drafting/architectural firm, they will put your design into building plan form, so the contractor and crews can build it exactly as you want it.

By using a drafting/architectural firm to draw up your building plans from your own design, the cost of the plans is dramatically reduced compared to plans that an architect might design from scratch. Depending on your level of knowledge, though, they may have to do some design changes for structural, safety, and/or zoning reasons. This may cost a little more, but still nothing like the cost of hiring an architect to oversee the whole project from start to finish.

Some builders may claim that they can build whatever you want without a set of building plans. Maybe they could, but I would not accept that. You will not know for sure exactly what you are getting before it goes up if you have no formal building plans. Also, there is nothing for the builder and crews to refer to. In order to be sure that they build it according to your specs, it is very important to have a set of actual building plans to approve or amend that were approved by a licensed drafting/architectural firm! Even if you purchase my building plans, I would consult an expert in your area to be sure my design meets zoning requirements in your area, and any other local considerations.

I had a wonderful builder who could have probably built our house from a sketch on a match book! But I still wouldn't have considered taking a chance on anything except real building plans. My builder recommended a good company that he had worked with frequently, and they were very helpful. I paid them on an hourly basis for just what I needed them to draw, and the cost was very reasonable. But you need to do your own homework and find the professionals that you feel will best meet your needs. Be sure to check references when choosing your builder/contractor and your architectural/drafting firm!

I have always called my building plans "blueprints", but now stand corrected. They are not called blueprints any more, nor are they blue. So I will now refer to the ones that a draftsman draws up as "building plans", and the ones I draw on graph paper as "floor plans".

Floor plans. After we bought our lot, the first thing we did was consult an engineering firm to get the lot surveyed. They plotted the lot within its legal description, and then added the elevation lines (altitude above sea level), showing the way the lot sloped and in what direction. We also requested that they mark where every tree was on the lot. There were two dogwoods and a cedar that I wanted to design around, because I didn't want to take them out. We also needed the elevations so we could plan whether a walk-out basement was reasonable.

After getting the plotted drawing, I made copies and started playing with it, preserving the original. The scale of the drawing was, I think, ten feet per inch, maybe twenty feet per inch. I don't remember now, but it was on a regular 8 ½ by 11 sheet of paper, so very easy to work with. I purchased graph paper tablets in the same size and counted out squares to get my measurements to scale.

At first, I was just playing around with what part of the lot we wanted the house to sit on – closer to the lake or closer to the road? I drew in the required set-backs, easements, and the government take line for the lake's flood plain. Then I just moved the house around to see where we might want it, which way it would face, etc. We knew it would be years before we could afford to build, so it was all just a pipe dream. But so much fun to imagine!

The road frontage on our lot was very limited. Therefore, the driveway location was pretty much decided for us. It had to come in where the road frontage was located. I could turn the driveway whichever way I wanted to put the garage, but there were really only two options for the garage placement relative to the driveway and road frontage. So the position of the house was pretty well dictated by the road frontage on one side and the lake on the other side.

The garage and main entrance to the house needed to be relative to the driveway, and the "rooms with a view" needed to be placed on the lake side, so that's where I started. I naturally wanted the living areas and master bedroom to have the best lake views. Then I only needed to figure out which rooms could be put on the front uphill side without the view. I chose the guest bedrooms, garage, and formal dining room to be the rooms on the front of the house that could do without the lake view. The master bedroom, family room/kitchen, and "man cave"/office all got the stunning water front vistas.

As you develop your floor plan, you will have a 2D representation on paper of where the rooms will be in relation to each other. A 2D (two dimensional) representation is what you see in magazines and floor plan books showing the layout of the house as it would look from above (looking at the "floor" space, literally). This stage of the design takes no décor, materials, or color into account. You can simply draw a rectangle on graph paper, and start from there. You can have each square represent 1 foot, 2 feet, or 5 feet, depending on how much detail you want to include.

I worked with the literal "floor" plan for the majority of my designs. I didn't work on any of the elevations (what the outside of the house or a wall would look like while standing in front of it) until I was completely done with the 2D floor plan layout. I did lay it out from the beginning with the vaulted ceilings in the center of the house in mind, but that is the only elevation I had pictured at that point.

I didn't worry too much about my roof lines until after I had the layout pretty well mapped out. That is maybe the backwards way to do it, but that is how it worked for me. When it came time to work on the roof line, it wasn't too difficult, and the draftsman did most of that work.

One thing I had a choice on was the roof pitch. Our house looks huge from the outside because we have a really steep roof pitch. It looks like it should be a two-story, but it is just because of the high roof line. I wanted a steep roof pitch so that there would never be a problem with unusually large snow loads, as seems to be happening more frequently around here. I had also heard horror stories about ice damming when a big snow melts off the roof, so wanted to prevent that. You may want to ask about snow loads in your area relative to the roof pitch you choose. I'm sure our high roof pitch was more expensive, but it does give the house a grand appearance. Please, if you run into questions you can't answer, be sure to consult the experts in your local area.

CHAPTER THREE

SIZE DOES MATTER!

What kind of home are you wanting? A large, sprawling home for lots of kids? A smaller, more efficient home for retirement? Do you want a walk-out basement? An attic? Do you need an outdoor entertainment area near the kitchen? Or a nice play yard for the kids where you can see them easily?

How many bedrooms do you need? An art or writing studio? Music room? Do you work from home? Would you need public spaces for clients? Space for a pool table? Would you want a three-car garage? Porches or decks? Formal living and/or dining areas? Family room? Theater/media room? Do you enjoy entertaining? Do you host lots of overnight guests? How much square footage are you willing to clean? Do you have any special hobbies that would need specific extra space or storage?

While you are designing the rough layout of your house on your lot, don't forget to keep within the required set-backs for your zoning area. I left a good 2 to 5 feet extra in addition to the required side yard set-backs on our house so no one could even think about jerking our permits or making us change something we had already built. Your builder will usually confirm these types of requirements for you, but don't forget to ask!

When deciding on how big your house should be, there are obviously lots of factors to consider. And you want to be sure you have no regrets after completion. Your budget may restrict the size you design, but you must be sure there will be adequate space to meet your needs, if it is truly to be your "dream home"! You also don't want it to be so extravagant that your spaces are inefficient and wasteful. If you design it to be too large, you may take away from convenience and cohesiveness. Sometimes, smaller and more efficient may win out over spacious and grand. Again, just give it enough thought that you are confident in your decisions.

If you do a lot of entertaining, then you will probably want a very open floor plan with good traffic planning and lots of space for people to circulate between the kitchen and living areas. Do you need more than one living area? A wet bar? Do you need a formal dining room? Or will a kitchen table or bar with stools work for your lifestyle?

Most homes these days should have space for an office, and many people want a spare bedroom for guests. If you decide to combine these two functions in one room, be sure to design the dimensions to accommodate all the functions and furniture you will need. Don't forget storage for those things you won't want sitting out when guests are present. I always thought a Murphy bed would be cool for guests, but decided they were too expensive when it came time to build. Air beds work great for temporary guests, as long as you allow enough floor space for them in your designs.

Stairs? Basement? How many stories do you want? Does anyone in your family have a problem with stairs? With our age, I knew I didn't want to have to negotiate stairs. Therefore, we have no stairs or even steps inside the house, no stairs to enter the house, and no steps from the garage into the kitchen. We do have stairs down from the deck out back, but that's the only place. That way, our house is also wheelchair accessible, if we ever need that in the future.

I originally wanted a basement, but we ended up with not quite enough fall on the lot to put in a walk-out basement without adding a lot of cost. I also realized that if I put the guest "wing" in the basement, I would still have to negotiate the stairs to clean it. I would also need to gather laundry and bedding after guests had been here. So that's why the "L" in the front of the house. That is where I put the guest wing instead of in the basement.

However, we did have enough fall on the lot to put a huge storage area under the house, and access it with double doors, kind of like a carriage house. It is unique and oh, so practical! The "crawl" space under our house is actually "walk-in" space. It is all graveled, so works great for storage of everything from trailers, golf cart and lawn mowers to storage tubs and boxes, as well as a "fraidy hole" if we ever need it for tornado warnings.

A two-story house is usually cheaper than a one-story house of the same square footage. This is because the "footprint" and foundation of the two-story house is so much smaller than spreading all that square footage out in a single story. Think of a high rise in New York. Then think of all that square footage spread out on ground level, and you can see how much more expensive it would be to spread it all out. That's why you can get more square footage for your money if you build up instead of out.

Many people may prefer two stories, or at least a basement, for this very reason. A stairway going up can add a lot of visual and architectural interest to a floor plan, if that's your thing. It also automatically separates your public areas from the more private ones. A basement may be a must for some people who want storm protection, added storage, or an additional entertainment area. I prefer the ranch style with everything on one floor, but everyone has their own tastes. Just be sure you think it through and know what you want ahead of time.

Room size and number. Next, you need to decide on the number of bedrooms you need, how large those bedrooms should be, where they will be in relation to each other and the rest of the house, and the purposes for each bedroom. What size bed(s) will you have in each room? Dressers? Desks? Built-ins? Closets? And don't forget to allow space for getting around in the room after furniture is placed. You don't want to stub toes or have to squeeze past the dresser to get to your side of the bed. By the way, I don't like placing beds against the wall because it makes them harder to make. Again, just my preference.

While you are planning this, it is a good idea to think about the re-sale value you are creating and what would appeal to the most people if and when you ever sell the house. You obviously want it to serve your needs specifically, but you also need to be practical. Something really outlandish might really hurt your chances of reselling your house for a fair price when the time comes.

The size of each bedroom may be critical, depending on your individual needs. I would personally not build any bedroom smaller than 10' X 10', and that is still pretty small. 12' X 14' makes a good size, with maybe a little larger for a master bedroom. These dimensions do NOT include the closet(s) or bathroom. Our master bedroom is 15' X 20', and that is very spacious and suits us well. I personally would not want any larger than that. But, again, you need to decide what sizes you can live with, the purposes and people that will occupy which rooms, and how much furniture and storage space/closets you need to put in each room.

My daughter is a massage therapist. If she chose to run her business out of her home, she could put a massage table in one of her bedrooms. But if planning something like this, don't forget to figure out not only how much room you need for the table, but also how much free room (around all sides of the table) is necessary to stand or sit while giving a massage. And if you need storage cabinets in the room, or chairs, hooks for clothes, etc., be sure to take this into account when planning the space needed. You would also want to consider access to a bathroom nearby and maybe access to the area from outside the house.

If you want a large dining room table, you must not only plan for the size of the table and chairs, but the space needed around it on all sides to get in and out of the chairs, serve food, clear plates, etc. And if you want some wall décor or a china cabinet, for instance, you will want to allow space for that without conking your head or squeezing by a corner. Same with a pool table. Not only will you need space for the table, but space around it for the sticks when actually playing. And if you want any seating or storage in the room, those furniture pieces cannot interfere with those trying to play pool. You may also need to consider the weight of a pool table or other special items in various rooms. You may need extra support under your floors, for example, if you want a pool table, water bed, or large jetted bathtub.

Our master bedroom is oversized to accommodate a sitting area and t.v. This was very high on our list of priorities. But our guest rooms are very small. Since this was our retirement home and the kids were grown and gone, we didn't need full size extra bedrooms. In our case, they were intended to be just sleeping rooms, because the kids or guests would spend most of their time in the living areas visiting with family and friends. Our small spare rooms would not be big enough for a teenager, for example, who might spend a lot of time in their room and want to have friends over. Little did I know that two of my adult children would move back in within a year of building my dream house!?! Oh, well, best not make the spare rooms TOO comfortable!

Buyers might turn down our house someday because of those small extra bedrooms. But I needed to consider the total size vs. cost of the house, and the extra bedrooms were one place I could cut down on square footage. However, my floor plan is designed to easily expand those two rooms by simply moving out one wall, without having to change any roof lines or go back to the drawing board. Any floor plan you like can be amended to fit your specific needs.

Our "game room" has a big screen t.v., game table and chairs, theater seating for 2, a small desk, and a day bed with a trundle for extra sleeping space. It is in the "guest wing" with the two small spare bedrooms and an oversized guest bath with double sinks. When we retired, we wanted to have a house at the lake that the kids and grandkids would want to come visit. That way, we would get to see them more often, and it would not be a "boring trip to grandma's house". When no one is visiting, we can close off the guest wing and live in our part of the house, saving money on utilities. But when kids, grandkids, or other guests are here, the flow works great, just like I had pictured!

I think it is nice to have a small formal living room near the entry (even though we don't have one in this house). This room can be used for reading, visiting with friends who stop by, or entertaining. Without a t.v., you can make a rule that the formal living room always stays clean and uncluttered. Then the larger family room adjacent to the kitchen could be used for t.v. watching and family time. Toys and other debris may often be scattered in the family room, but not everyone will see that clutter unless you invite them in.

I designed our "dream home" to have a formal dining room, but no formal living room. We have a very large family room/kitchen combination, and with the game room for the kids and guests, that's all we needed. We never "entertain" as such, so did not feel that a formal living room was necessary. But when we do have a crowd, the formal dining room is wonderful for all to sit and eat together. Again, it all depends on your personal preferences and lifestyle.

We do have our kids, grandkids and close friends visiting frequently. We have had as many as twenty staying at our house at one time! In this case, you have every bed, sofa, chair and floor taken up with bodies, often in sleeping bags! So I designed built-in window seats under the windows in the living room (on either side of the fireplace) for extra sleeping space and storage for toys for the great-grandkids. And there is some open floor space in nearly every room for air beds, so no one has to step over anyone to get to the bathroom or kitchen. I love having a house full of happy people, and our space works great for whomever comes to visit!

As we age, having "company" can be tiring, so we designed our spaces for maximum convenience for both us and our guests. We have the family room and kitchen area for our space and usual routine, and the game room is available for anyone else that comes to visit. If the kids want to play video games or watch something on t.v. other than what we are watching, they can go in the other room, have their own space, and feel right at home. That way, we don't get too tuckered out by our space and routine being compromised when others are here. It works out very well for our needs.

These are the kinds of things you can come up with to customize your home and fit your lifestyle. Just be sure to allow enough room for whatever activities are important to you. Size does matter!

CHAPTER FOUR

LOCATION! LOCATION! LOCATION!

B efore you can go very far on your floor plan layout and design, you must have a place to build it. However, before you choose a lot, you must know approximately what size the "footprint" of your house will be. You also need to consider what features you want to include, such as a walk-out basement. That is why I waited until Chapter 4 to discuss location. Chapter 2 covers layout and design, and Chapter 3 discusses size considerations.

If you haven't chosen your lot yet, you have no limitations on your home design or size. You still have the freedom to design your house any way you like and then pick the lot to accommodate it. If you do already have your building site, congratulations and good luck! However, care must be used in designing your home to fit the lot, zoning and set-back requirements, and topography (lay of the land, elevations, slope, etc).

In determining which property to buy to build your house on, there are several things to consider. What direction does the lot face? Which location will give you the best sun and energy efficiency? Which will provide the best natural lighting for different rooms and purposes? How far is the location from work, school, leisure activities? Which locations are the best value for your budget? Is the size of the lot sufficient for your needs? How are the local schools? Traffic? Security? How is the water pressure in the neighborhood?

You need to consider traffic on the street, both for children and pets, but also for backing out of your driveway on a busy morning. And will noisy traffic take away from your enjoyment of your morning coffee on the deck? What about water drainage? Sloped enough for a walk-out basement? Flat enough for a nice play yard?

Do you prefer to be "where the action is" or secluded and private? In a family oriented area or mostly retired people? Are restrictive covenants for the neighborhood consistent with what you want to build? What kind of scenic views do you want from the windows? Trees? Hills? Water? City scape? Rooftops? Cemetery? Neighbors?

Depending on your budget, all these things can dramatically affect the price of your lot or building site, but at least you should be aware of them before you purchase. I would think that most people who are building for the first time would not think to consider all of the above factors. The whole purpose of this book is to eliminate as many unpleasant surprises as possible, before it is too late to change.

Using a reputable Realtor and a well-referenced Builder has many advantages, starting with the knowledge and experience they have in answering a lot of the questions you will have before you get started. They may also be more familiar with the local area in which you are considering purchasing a building site. Most Realtors will know about the types of neighborhoods and local schools in their area, if you are moving in from another locale. A reputable Builder can probably tell you about the ground you are building on as well (rocky, sandy, clay, lime, etc.), and the best type of foundation to use.

We knew we wanted something near our favorite lake and recreational area to retire to. We have both always loved nature and the outdoors, fishing and boating, hiking and camping. Our lake-front lot, facing east so the deck would be shaded from the hot afternoon sun, with a private boat dock and 48 trees on ½ acre, was perfect for our needs. Since we were not going to build until retirement, we didn't need to consider proximity to schools or work, and our requirements were much smaller than would be true for most people. But mostly, we just got lucky and the only property we looked at seemed to be a perfect match for our needs.

While you are shopping for a location to build on, don't forget the possibility of severe weather or other natural disasters (blizzards, floods, mudslides, tornadoes, hurricanes, earthquakes, forest fires, etc.) relative to where you want to live, and plan your structure accordingly. Local building codes may be less strict in rural areas, but those codes are there for a reason. Your structure should meet or exceed the going regulations in your state, county and nearby towns.

Knowledge of normal weather conditions for the area you are looking at is also important. In a colder climate, you might want all Southern exposure windows for all day sun to help with heating your home. In a hot and dry climate, you may want a Northern or Eastern exposure. In snowy climates, the slope of the street and driveway for getting around in bad weather should be considered. If you've ever seen flood damage, you know not to buy in an area prone to high or standing water, or only a few feet up from a creek or river bottom that could flash flood. In tornado alley, you probably don't want a house on the top of a hill or in the middle of a large flat valley.

If you are older, you should consider the accessibility of medical and other services you may need. If you get a chance before you buy, you should ask neighbors about schools, utilities, water pressure, security, etc. Location! Location! Location! It really is key to planning the right spot for your needs.

CHAPTER FIVE

THE NITTY GRITTY: FOUNDATION AND UTILITIES

I am so glad that I had such a wonderful builder! I had no clue about how the foundation, ductwork, plumbing, wiring, and all the other things that must go under a house and in the walls needed to be engineered. When we added on to our home in Oklahoma, it was much easier to tie into existing pipes and wiring than building from scratch! I had the design of my dream home, and layout of all my rooms ready, and could really envision what it would all look like. But I hadn't given much thought to the nuts and bolts of creating it all from scratch. It was fascinating to watch it all come together.

Footings, foundation, septic and sewer. Depending on the lay of the land on your building site, you may have a choice to build on a concrete slab, or have a crawl space under the house. I prefer a concrete slab. It just seems more solid to me. However, if you build on a slab and a pipe breaks in or under it, you are in a heap of trouble!

Even though I prefer a slab, we didn't have that option here. Our lot sloped too much for a slab. Obviously, the garage is on a slab and so is the front porch. But the rest is over a crawl space. The nice thing about that is, since it does slope so much, we were able to put a lot of storage area under the house, accessing it from the back of the house through a set of walk-through doors.

You have to decide what you want in the way of a foundation, but your selection of building sites may determine that for you. Your builder can also help with those decisions, and should know the best type of foundation to use for your area. Our builder also lined the entire crawl space with thick plastic sheeting covered by clean 1" gravel. That makes the whole space cleaner, drier and more useable for dry storage.

As you finalize your floor plans, you must take them to an architectural/drafting firm to put them into building plan form. This is what your builder/contractor and all the contract crews and tradesmen will use to actually build your house. Your draftsman will make several pages of plans for your house. One version is obviously the actual floor plan for building. But there will also be a version for the roof line, one for the foundation, one for electrical, and so on.

As the building is going up, you can make small changes and upgrades, but the footings and foundation structure obviously cannot be changed once you begin. I guess you could change them at great expense, but not realistically. Just be sure to take your time and be sure you are ready before you actually break ground.

Hopefully, your builder will double-check with you and clarify what you want at each step of the process, as ours did. He had all the "know-how" needed to pull off what I had designed, and luckily he tried very hard to build exactly what I had envisioned. He checked with me frequently and asked all the right questions so that the final outcome was what I expected it to be like, only better! He seemed to know when to clarify something to be sure he built true to my vision. It was really awesome. I think it is imperative that you choose a builder that will work with you easily and communicate clearly.

Since we are in a rural setting, we had to have a septic tank. The septic tank was in and filled with water long before we broke ground to start building! And as they poured the footings, holes were allowed for sewer and pipes to enter and exit the foundation in various places. Once this is done, there's no going back! So you have to make sure all decisions are made and final before pouring any footings.

Speaking of the septic tank, we chose to have a larger tank than minimum requirements for the size of the house we were building. We also added ample lateral lines to be sure our system could cope when we had a large influx of guests. If you have to use a septic system, keep in mind that they usually only last about 20 – 30 years. Therefore, make sure you have enough property to adequately serve your needs over the long haul. Most of you won't have to worry about that, as sewer systems are usually available in most areas. I just didn't want you to forget this part while you were still in the designing phase.

By the way, Erma was right! The grass really IS greener over the septic tank (or at least over the lateral lines)! You may not be old enough to know who Erma Bombeck was, but I just thought I would throw it in for a little humor!

Utilities. You probably won't have to think too much about accessing your utilities – your builder will know how to connect to existing water lines, sewer and electric. He/she will also get all the necessary permits for doing so. However, your plumbing decisions and bathroom locations need to be set in stone before pouring the footings. And you have several decisions to make about the types of utilities you want to choose.

Water sources and water pressure are two things you should research when buying your building site. Water pressure can be poor in certain housing areas, and your potential neighbors will be able to tell you how their water pressure is. If it is a problem in your neighborhood, it can be very difficult to get officials or the water company in your area to remedy the problem.

Your water sources may be city water, a well, or a coop. Be sure to check into these things before you begin. We have plenty of water pressure, and good drinking water. However, we chose to put a whole-house water filter on our water supply, just to be safe. We also had to install a heavy-duty whole-house water softener because our water is very hard in this area. If you have hard water and don't use a softener, your appliances that use water (dishwasher, coffee pot, clothes washer, etc.) will have a much shorter life span because of the minerals in the water that will clog them up. You may also wish to check into a rain water catchment system if you are going "green".

For your heating source, clothes dryer, cooking, and hot water heater, you need to decide on gas/propane, solid fuel, or all electric. Checking on these items may make a huge difference in your quality of life and utility costs over time and warrants some study before you make your final decisions. We were accustomed to natural gas in Oklahoma, but that was not an option here. We had to go with either total electric, or have a propane tank. Since I insisted on a gas cook-top, we went with propane. I'm glad we did, because I now also have a gas fireplace insert which is gorgeous. I also think our water heater and furnace are less expensive than electric would have been.

Electrical power depends on the neighborhood your property is in. Most newer housing areas have buried electric lines, which are much preferable to overhead lines! This may be something else you want to check on before you buy your building site. Your HVAC (heat and air) unit type and location should also be planned early on, and should be centrally located in the house. It can go in a closet, under the house, or in the attic, but should be near the center of the house for best efficiency and even temperatures throughout the house.

The same is true for your hot water heater. We chose a super-efficient gas water heater, but did consider the on-demand tankless units as well. They reportedly don't last as long as regular hot water tanks, but are much more energy efficient. And you need to consider the location and efficiency of your plumbing lines, as I discussed in chapter 2 on design, and again in the following section. Please review this information to save a bundle on plumbing costs.

Plumbing. Plumbing and pipes are very expensive, and so is your plumber's time. As you play with laying out your rooms in relation to each other, keep this in mind to save money. It is much cheaper to build if you put your plumbing areas near each other. Pipes that have to go all the way across your house to a lone bathroom will cost more than if you run them to only one or two areas of your home. If you cluster the rooms needing water, you could save quite a bit in construction costs. For instance, if you have the laundry room backing up to the kitchen or a bathroom, that will save money.

The more spread out your plumbing fixtures are, the more expensive it will be to build. So if you place bathrooms back to back, or a bathroom adjacent to the kitchen, for example, you will be making more efficient use of your construction dollars. The pipes running through the walls will be more efficient if you are supplying two rooms at one time through the same wall than if you have to plumb two separate walls a ways apart. Again, it takes quite a bit of time and consideration to make your design most efficient.

The following illustration shows some examples of efficient placement of plumbing. Note that the water areas are more central and the living and other areas that don't need water are more peripheral in the designs. Example "a" shows how the laundry room and two bathrooms can be clustered together along one outside wall. Example "b" shows how a 3 bedroom house could be configured fairly efficiently.

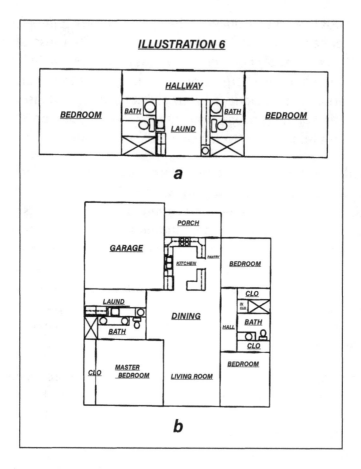

Think of all your water and sewer lines as if they were $1000 per foot and plan accordingly. That is obviously NOT what they cost, but it is a nice round number for realizing how the costs can add up. Pipes need to be run into the house from your water supply line outside, and then go to each sink, toilet, tub, shower, water heater, dishwasher, clothes washer, and even the refrigerator (if you have an ice maker). Then drains must run from each water-using device to your sewer lines and outside.

You also need to consider the distance your water use areas are from your water heater. You probably don't want to run your shower for 5 minutes waiting for your water to heat up! Placing your water heater and water use areas strategically in your overall design will help with this problem significantly and increase your efficiency.

In my floor plan, I could not consolidate all water uses as efficiently as I would have liked because of the way I wanted my rooms to flow into each other. But I did take this into account as much as possible. After the fact, I now know that I would move the mechanical closet in the garage to a more central location within the house. Then I could make the pantry much smaller, and put the half bath in that location, allowing room for my kitchen table in the nook.

CHAPTER SIX

BUILDING, MATERIALS, AND "GOING GREEN"

When you build a house, your builder/contractor will usually give you an estimated cost per square foot of what your house will cost to build, in your part of the country. That estimate includes not only all the materials to be used, but also all labor, permits, carpenters, plumbers, electricians, and so on. Your builder/contractor's fee is part of that total cost, too. His/her fee is usually made up of either a flat fee added to the actual cost, or a percentage of what it actually costs to build the house. Your builder will probably do some of the work him/herself, and supervise all of it. But much of the work is delegated to professional tradesmen and crews that the builder contracts with to complete the work. That is why he is called a "contractor".

Speaking of cost, when you take out your building loan, your lender will not give you the money up front to build your house. The lender (bank or mortgage company) will usually advance you certain amounts at a time. You will then give the builder advances as you go along, to pay for different phases of the building process. With our house, we set up a separate checking account specifically for the building project, and the bank would advance us portions of the total loan as needed. They would deposit a certain amount into our construction account, then we would pay the builder or vendors from that account. That way, everything was easy to balance regularly and account for every penny spent as we went along.

The way our bank operated its construction loans, which I really appreciated, was that each time the builder asked for another advance, the bank required that he submit all receipts for actual expenses paid from the previous advance. They would not make the next advance until he had given them all receipts and records of all expenses to date. This is for your protection (and the bank's), to be sure that your money is used as it was intended, and you have a home to show for it when all is completed. Without these assurances, some unscrupulous builder could keep your money without paying off all vendors or tradesmen, and they could come after you for the money! This is another reason that you should get plenty of references and know that you can trust your builder/contractor.

Upgrades. At the time we built our house, our builder estimated that it would cost about $100 per square foot to build. Because I insisted on so many custom features (especially built-in cabinetry) and high-end materials, we went way over that budget.

Some builders may give you an "allowance" for certain things you will pick out, so you will stay in budget. If your carpet allowance, for instance, is $3 per square foot and you pick out a carpet that costs $4 per square foot, you just went over budget. You must either pay that difference over the allotted budget, or choose something below your allowance in another area to make up for the extra cost. If you go over budget on the materials that you pick out, it is NOT included in the original estimated cost. YOU pay the difference! You must keep in close touch with your builder to be sure you are staying within budget.

My husband and I decided that we really couldn't afford hardwood floors, so chose a reasonably priced quality carpet instead. Then our builder took us to see one of his other houses that he had just finished building. One of the features in that house was a solid wood cedar ceiling. Northern White Cedar, to be exact. It was just so beautiful that we couldn't resist adding that feature to our vaulted ceilings in the living areas of our house. I had planned on ordinary sheet rock ceilings, but we both agreed to add this upgrade.

If we thought we could NOT afford hardwood floors, what made us think we COULD afford hardwood ceilings!?! The impact of that choice is phenomenal in our house and adds so much to the grandeur of the vaulted ceilings. However, it added an equally phenomenal amount to our overall budget!

The Northern White Cedar ceilings were an impulse upgrade. We are not sorry that we made that choice because we truly love it, but it did raise the total budget significantly. Just remember, if you need to stick to a budget, you must resist impulse upgrades during the building process! And you will be tempted more than once, believe me!

The temptations to upgrade your materials and features may be pretty frequent, so beware. It is easy to think that "just this one" special upgrade won't hurt. But those costs add up quickly! On the other hand, if your budget isn't too strict, the upgrades that you can afford during the process are one thing that make the house uniquely yours, and can add to your overall satisfaction with your finished product.

Materials. You should get to choose, within reason, all the materials your builder will use. However, choosing those materials will most likely begin with your builder. Does he or she usually build wood frame (stick-built) houses? Are you considering pre-manufactured housing? Concrete block? Metal framing? Do you want a brick exterior? Stone? Siding? What kind of roofing material do you prefer? Most people use the traditional stick-built house with one of the usual exterior materials, but I just wanted you to be aware that there are many other options out there to consider.

Will you prefer the usual sheet rock walls on the interior, or do you want more unique wall treatments like wood, stone, brick, glass, or other surfaces? You can make quite an impact in décor with surfaces other than sheet rock, but they will probably add considerably to your total budget. A well-chosen paint and tasteful wall décor on sheet rock can be exquisite and much less costly.

Flooring is another area you should give quite a bit of thought to. There are many choices from carpet to hardwood, laminates to bamboo, vinyl tile to travertine. Stained concrete is another good choice, depending on your tastes and lifestyle. Hardwood is very popular right now, but I think it is harder to maintain and keep it looking good.

I like carpet underfoot in bedrooms and family areas, as it is softer and warmer. But many people think that carpet holds too much dirt and allergens. If you do choose carpet, you should use a high grade if you want it to hold up to years of wear and tear. Depth and softness of carpet should also be considered, because thicker carpet is harder to walk on for babies and the elderly. Obviously, carpet is NOT appropriate in kitchens or bathrooms – ever!

We have stone tiles on all of our floors that are not carpeted, but it is a very hard surface, as is stained concrete. If you fall or drop something on it, things and people are more likely to break! But I love my floors and they will be here long after I am gone! There are cushioned tiles that look like stone, and laminates that look like hardwood, and they are usually much less expensive. However, you will need to replace those materials more often as they do not hold up like hardwood or stone.

Countertops are another big expense that you should research before choosing your surfaces. Do your homework and compare the pros and cons on granite, corian, quartz, marble, concrete, and all the other surfaces out there. The newer laminates may even be in the running for you, since they are so much less expensive than solid surface materials. They are of much higher quality, durability and appearance now, too, than the old laminate surfaces of the 60's and 70's.

Kitchen countertops are probably most important, but bathroom vanities and other surfaces also need to be given careful thought. So you should get information on all the materials available and then decide which one(s) to use in which areas of your home. I would advise you to go to several merchants to get started, as each store usually only carries 2 to 3 brands or options for countertops. They will gladly give you their opinion on which surface they think is better! Then you can also research the options online, if you need more information, before making your choice.

Everyone seems to want granite these days, but after you research the subject, you may find other solid surface materials preferable. Does your choice of countertop material stand up to heat if you set a hot pan on it right off the stove or out of the oven? Does your choice of material need to be sealed regularly to keep out moisture and bacteria? Does it stain or scratch easily? Chip or crack? These are the questions you have to answer to decide what you can live with. And there is a huge price difference between materials, with the most expensive not necessarily having all the qualities that are important to you. Again, you need to balance pros and cons of each to make the choices that are right for you. Don't just go with the most popular at the time.

Plumbing fixtures vary a great deal, also. I have a "thing" about fiberglass or acrylic tubs, shower surrounds, and sinks. I think fiberglass, resin, or acrylic tubs, for instance, look great when new, but do not hold up well over time. They are MUCH less expensive than the traditional cast iron tubs coated with ceramic, but do not resist stains and scratches over time nearly as well as ceramic over cast iron.

My master bath jetted tub was EXTREMELY expensive, as I insisted on ceramic over cast iron instead of a fiberglass or acrylic tub, and I also over-did on the jets. But I am so happy that I went with the cast iron! It will look like new nearly forever if I take care of it and don't scrub too hard with abrasive cleaners. On the contrary, fiberglass does not clean as easily and will NOT stay new-looking for very many years. Same for shower surrounds. I much prefer ceramic tile in showers, but it is expensive. We ended up with faux marble on our shower walls, which is much less expensive and holds up nearly as well as ceramic tile, with fewer grouted joints to leak.

Then you have toilets, sinks, and faucets to pick out. I would not buy a toilet that was not solid china. That is what most are, but there are still many choices in style and function to choose from. Faucets vary greatly in style and price as well, so it may take you a while to find what suits your tastes and budget.

Sinks also come in all kinds of shapes, sizes and materials. I love Corian, because it does not stain, cleans up easily, and looks great for years. China sinks are pretty inexpensive and look nice long term, but they can break if something hard is dropped on them. We actually have a white acrylic sink in our laundry room that has so far held up well. We ended up with manufactured marble for our bathroom sinks and vanity tops because it was cheaper. However, it scratches pretty easily, so you have to clean it carefully. Again, it depends on your budget and the pros and cons you consider for each material.

Doors, windows, appliances, cabinets and hardware (cabinet handles, door knobs, towel bars, to name a few) are some other types of materials and products you will need to pick out. It can be a daunting task and may take you a while to choose all the things you will need, so be sure to allow enough time to look at your options. Your builder will probably have some stores and vendors he recommends, so you can start there. Just be prepared to spend quite a bit of time shopping, whether in person or online!

"Going Green" Another consideration when choosing materials is whether it is important to you to consider your impact on the environment. The resources you choose to use for building materials may consist of: (1) non-renewable natural resources, (2) renewable resources, and (3) recycled products. The efficiency of your home and the appliances you choose can also have varying affects on the environment after you are done building and move in.

I am not taking sides on this issue, just giving you the information. If you really feel strongly about the environment, I would encourage you to do your own research on how you can best go about reducing your environmental impact. For the most part, going green will be much more expensive than using traditional materials. Again, it all depends on your own personal convictions and budget.

If "going green" is your choice, I see two distinct phases to the process. The first is in the materials you choose to use while building and their impact on the environment. The second is the number of resources you affect after your home is built (water and energy used, trash and sewage produced, etc.). Going green means doing everything you can to preserve the environment and reduce your "carbon footprint" on the earth. Your "carbon footprint" is what you and your lifestyle leave behind from your mere existence.

People and animals breathe in oxygen and release carbon dioxide (CO_2) when they breathe out. Trees and plants do the opposite. They "breathe" in carbon dioxide and release oxygen into the atmosphere. Trees also "filter" the air to some degree, reducing pollutants. Thus, when trees are cut to build your house, you are reducing the oxygen that those trees might have returned to the air we breathe. That's one reason why environmentalists are so vocal about preserving trees and forests.

Every time you burn anything (wood, gasoline in your car, oil or gas to heat your house, etc.), you add carbon to the atmosphere, in one form or another. Wood and paper come from trees. Most plastics originate from crude oil by-products. And nearly all manufacturing processes produce carbon in some form. So that is what is meant by your "carbon footprint". If you use lots of wood, plastics, paper, gasoline, etc., in your lifetime or while building your house, for instance, you are increasing the carbon footprint that you leave on the environment.

"Green" materials. Lots of importance is being placed now on reducing our use of non-renewable resources such as oil and fossil fuels, metals, stone, etc. Since use of these materials depletes those resources in the environment, it stands to reason that we will someday run out of those resources. That is one reason that recycling is becoming so popular. The theory is that if we re-use those resources that have already been taken from the earth, it will reduce the demand to harvest additional resources from the land.

Renewable resources are products that we can replace and "renew" the supply of. Things that we can grow easily and quickly (fast-growing corn for fuel, bamboo in place of wood, etc.) are a good example of renewable resources. Oil, gas, plastics, stone, granite, minerals and metals are not renewable. Therefore, they should be used in limited amounts if you wish to "go green".

Bamboo, which grows quickly, is a very popular renewable resource to use in place of hardwood floors, for instance. It is more easily renewable than wood. Trees can be cultivated and planted, thus are renewable, but they are slow growing. And hardwoods (cherry, walnut, etc.) are slower to grow than softer woods like pine. That's why hardwoods are also more expensive.

There are a lot of products on the market now, with more being developed every day, that use a combination of recycled materials along with renewable resources. Many of these are very durable and desirable, but the "jury is still out" on some that still need to be around longer to be "tried and true". Sorry about all the clichés, but if the shoe fits...

Another consideration is the use of CFL (compact fluorescent) light bulbs. They cost a lot more than incandescent light bulbs (the kind we always used to use), but are supposed to last much longer and save energy. However, they are also toxic to the environment if not disposed of properly. So you need to balance all that out in your decision making. I personally have not had good experience with the CFL bulbs lasting as long as they claim they should.

Your builder and/or architect will have their own opinions and experience in the area of which materials to use, but it is ultimately your decision. You should probably consult with a variety of "experts" before choosing what you think is the best way to go. You also have to balance the cost vs. benefit of whatever you choose.

Efficiency and conservation. The second phase of "going green" is the efficiency of what you end up with after you are done building and move in. Insulation materials, appliances, heating and cooling options, etc., all vary in their energy efficiency. Generally, the more efficient a product is, the more expensive it is. The most efficient appliances, for example, will save you money on your utility costs long term. However, they cost more up front to purchase in the short term. How much must you save in monthly costs to offset the added expense you put into the appliance to begin with? How many years will it take for you to recoup your added expense through monthly utility savings?

Are you most interested in efficiency ratings because of the amount of energy it will save for the environment, or are you more interested in the amount of money you will save by having higher efficiency? How much are you willing to increase your budget to reduce your impact on the environment and improve your energy efficiency?

The savings from solar and wind energy, I would think, would be the most significant, as these energy sources are essentially free and endless once you make the initial investment for them. As far as I know, harnessing these energy sources also has no negative impact on the environment. However, I do not know anything about the upkeep or repair history of these sources, so you would again need to do your own homework. I am obviously not the expert you would consult with these kinds of questions.

Geo-thermal energy is another area you might consider. There are geo-thermal heating and cooling units (very expensive but maybe worth it in the long run) that use the constant underground temperature of 55 - 60 degrees to help defray your heating and cooling costs. If we'd had the money, I would have been very interested in this fairly new technology.

Passive energy savings such as strategic tree planting have negligible cost yet universal application. Planting evergreens on the North side of your house will save on heating costs in winter, as they will protect your home somewhat from cold North winds. Deciduous trees (ones that lose their leaves in the winter) should be planted on the South and West sides of your house. That way, your house will be shaded from the hot summer sun, saving on air conditioning. And that same warming sun will be allowed through to warm the house during the winter when the leaves fall off the trees. Just be sure not to plant trees too close to your structure or where they might interfere with underground water, sewer, gas or electric lines.

Conservation of other resources, especially water, will be important in most areas. There are lots of choices in plumbing, toilets, shower heads, washers, etc., that will conserve the amount of water you use in your home. Lighting is another subject entirely, and I will discuss that next, in Chapter 7. Your choices in doors and windows should also be high on your list for getting the most bang for your buck in cost and efficiency. I will address doors and windows in Chapter 8.

CHAPTER SEVEN

LIGHTING, ELECTRICAL, AND TECHNOLOGY

I still know very little about electrical systems, even with all I have learned over the years. Thank goodness for the wonderful professional tradesmen I have had the privilege of working with! They had to teach me a lot. But don't feel bad and don't be afraid to ask questions if you are not sure about something. If you don't ask questions and make sure you understand each other, you may end up with something that is not what you intended in your construction process. I hope your builder uses someone who will work well with you on your designs.

Electrical. Your builder will ask you, when the construction is to that point, to walk through the whole building site and decide on lighting, ceiling fan locations, electrical outlets, cable wiring, telephone lines, computer wiring, etc. He should also let you know where your breaker box will be located. There will most likely be an electrical plan in amongst your building plans, but this is usually just a place to start and is not carved in stone.

When you walk through the house with your builder, you should have already given a lot of thought to where you want your outlets, cable, lights and other wiring to go. If you haven't planned ahead on this, you may make some impulse decisions that either cost you more money or leave you without adequate wiring for your needs. This section will deal mostly with electrical outlets and where to put them. Please see the next section on cable and phone wiring, wi-fi, "smart house" technology, etc. I will address lighting last in this chapter.

Electrical outlets can be placed anywhere you want them, so be sure and picture how you might arrange your rooms so you can plan the most convenient places to put your outlets. If you have a sewing or craft table, for instance, you may want to put outlets for that wall above table level, so you don't have to crawl under the table to plug things in. I have one outlet next to the light switch in my sewing room to plug in the vacuum cleaner without having to bend over. This is really handy and I use it a lot. It costs x-amount for each outlet you put in, regardless of where you put it! It doesn't really cost any more to put them at 24 or 36" off the floor than it does to put them just above the baseboards. Planning ahead will give you lots of ideas to customize your outlets.

I had outlets put on each side of where my headboard was to go in the master bedroom, to allow for all the things that may set on my bedside tables. I also have a large low dresser with a make-up table in the center, so I put an outlet on either end of the dresser wall, above the level of the dresser top, so that it was easy to plug in things like my radio, make-up mirror, etc., without having to move the dresser to plug them in. These outlets are up about 24" off the floor instead of just above the baseboards. I also had electrical outlets put up under the bar in the kitchen, for plugging things in without having to bend over or stringing a cord across the bar.

It may seem like an overkill to some people, but I have at least one outlet on every wall in every room, and two outlets on longer walls. It is much better to have more available outlets than it is to use extension cords or power strips that could get overheated and cause a fire! I also have outlets built INTO the floor in the family room, on either end of where the sofa goes. That way, no cords have to drape across the traffic area to plug things into the wall.

I find it very difficult to get down on the floor any more, or to move furniture out from the wall to get to electrical wall outlets. That's why I like to have some at a higher level than usual. I have also lived in houses or apartments (and taught in schools) that did not have sufficient outlets for everything I needed to plug in. That's why I am so adamant about having outlets on every wall and planning ahead for everything you might foresee needing, both now and in the future.

I also have some outlets above my built-in china cabinet buffet in the dining room, and have used them for warming plates, fondue pots, etc. Just be sure that you don't end up with a room or wall that does not have what you need. Give it enough thought, so that you have an idea how you will arrange and use your furniture in each room, so the outlets will be where you will need them.

Cable, television, telephone and computer wiring. We
have enough wiring in our walls to light up New York, I think! I made sure every room had at least two cable locations for t.v. options, one or two telephone options, plenty of outlets near each one, cat 5 cable where needed, and low-voltage wiring for surround sound speakers in most rooms. By having two hook-ups in a room for t.v. cable, for instance, you allow for more flexibility in room arrangement and furniture placement.

You should have pretty much already decided where you think your television(s), telephones (if you have a land line), and computer wiring will go, before your builder asks where you want the internal wiring to go to support them. Our electrical wiring, telephone lines, satellite t.v., wi-fi, etc., were largely a joint effort between me and my husband, our builder, and at least three different electricians to make sure it would do what we wanted it to do. Be sure your experts are "expert" enough to know how to accomplish your goals, especially with all the new "smart house" technology, electronics, and computing bells and whistles which are becoming more and more popular. We probably have sufficient wiring for whatever we ever want to do, but it took quite a bit of planning.

We have our Wi-Fi center on top of one of the cabinets in the kitchen, where it is central to all rooms and the deck, accessible, yet out of sight. We did this, instead of putting it all in the computer room, to be sure that it would reach all areas in the house.

Lighting. Lighting is the one area where I wish I could have a "do-over"! This is where I think I made the most mistakes and have numerous regrets. I did do a lot right, but I also learned a lot about what I could have done better. First of all, I have too many lights and fixtures in most rooms, so spent lots of money I wouldn't have needed to spend. Second, I did not consider the amount of light each fixture would put out and the most efficient placement of each for best lighting, despite what I thought was clear planning.

I am happy with my fixtures and choices in general, but realized after the fact that I had spent way too much money without giving my actual lighting needs enough thought. All in all, I think my lack of experience in this area really showed. Consulting an architect would have been helpful, in hindsight. They have expertise in lighting as well, both natural and artificial, and its impact on all facets of the design. So I hope, if you have any doubt at all, that you will consult the experts. But that is another reason for writing this book. To share what I learned from experience and to assist others in designing their dream home successfully.

Oh, I did great on selecting beautiful light fixtures and chandeliers for the living areas that matched my décor fabulously. I found the most gorgeous pendant lights to hang over my island in the kitchen, which really make a wonderful statement. And I made sure to pick ceiling fans with light fixtures that pointed downward to make the bulbs easier to change. I was so pleased with our stylish purchases! What I didn't take into account was the types of light bulbs some of these fixtures used, and how much light they actually put out.

I worried more about the appearance of the fixtures I chose, and my décor, than about the practical and functional details that I should have taken into consideration.

My beautiful pendant lights over my kitchen island have very small, low-wattage light bulbs, so do not provide as much task lighting as I was expecting. The bulbs are also very expensive, at nearly $15.00 EACH to replace, nearly impossible to find in stores, and difficult to change in the fixtures! I also didn't put any light above my prep sink, where the island turns, so that part of the kitchen is rather dark to work in. A pot light there would have been perfect, and much less expensive.

My main kitchen light fixture matches the family room ceiling fan wonderfully, but I didn't realize I would be standing in my own light at most of my work stations. Looking back on it, I would eliminate the main kitchen hanging fixture all together, in favor of more pot lights in the kitchen ceiling. I would also have left the light fixture off of the ceiling fan.

In the family room, I have recessed (pot) lighting in all four corners, a lighted ceiling fan, AND a row of pretty mini-spotlights on each of the open wood beams to light up our gorgeous Northern White Cedar vaulted ceilings. Any ONE of these three light sources would have been sufficient! I think my favorite lights are the mini spotlights on the beams. They can be arranged to shine in whatever direction we choose, and I love them shining on the ceiling for indirect lighting. There's only one problem with those lights. I intentionally put them on the back side of the beams so they wouldn't be visible from the entry. That way, you would see the lighted area but would not see the actual fixtures. That was a brilliant idea in theory, but we rarely turn them on. They are on the side of the beams toward the fireplace, so they reflect horribly on our big screen t.v., which is mounted above the fireplace! If these light fixtures had been placed on the other side of the beams, that wouldn't be a problem.

Speaking of light reflections on the t.v. screen, the kitchen chandelier and the lighted ceiling fan also reflect badly when they are on. And the pot lights in the corners shine right in our eyes when we are trying to watch t.v.! So much for well-thought-out lighting! We have gotten used to it and it doesn't bother us any more, but I wish I had known this before I put the fixtures where I did!

I did pretty well in the closets and laundry room, picking attractive but reasonably priced fixtures in those areas. I am also pleased with the ceiling fans and fixtures I chose for the bedrooms and office. However, in the master bedroom, I put not only a lighted ceiling fan, but also recessed pot lights in all four corners! One or the other of these would have been plenty, especially since we have small lamps for our bedside tables. I love pot lights, but they are really not necessary in a bedroom. One overhead fixture would have been more than enough! I just went way overboard with the lights.

When you are picking out your fixtures, be sure and check the type of bulbs they use and their wattage. Bedrooms will probably be fairly easy, as you really don't need much task lighting in there. But your living areas, kitchen, and office need sufficient lighting for all the tasks you will undertake in those rooms. And think about how you will change light bulbs (and what they cost), as this may make a difference in what you choose. Pot lights are great, but some of the bulbs they use can be more expensive. Also, pot light bulbs are harder to change than in a hanging fixture, especially if you have high ceilings.

My dining room chandelier and matching entry light are awesome, and I did not overload the dining room with unnecessary fixtures. However, I wish I had put the chandelier and entry light on the same switch! There are four switches by the front door, and it is confusing to remember which switch turns on which lights. In the family room, there is a row of SIX light switches on one wall. It took us months to remember which switches operated which lights!

Really quite ridiculous. Hopefully, you can learn from my mistakes here and do a better job of planning yours!

Your light fixture/chandelier over your dining room table should hang low enough to light your table surface, but high enough to look under when you are standing around the table. There is a formula (though I don't remember what it is) for where your dining room chandelier should hang, but I like mine a little higher than that. I would put the bottom of the light fixture just above eye level of the tallest person in your household. You don't need to worry about walking under this fixture, because your table will be under it. If the fixture is centered in the room and the table will not necessarily be right under it, then I would raise the bottom of the fixture to at least 6'6", unless you have someone taller than that in your family.

In each of my bedrooms, the ceiling fan is operated by two separate switches. One for the fan, and one for the attached light. The lighted fans also operate on their own pull chains, but I like leaving these on and using the switches at the door. This is a nice feature, since those are the only switches in the bedrooms. In my master bedroom, I also put a second light switch beside my bed for our master bedroom pot lights, so I can turn them on or off without having to get out of bed. That was my builder's suggestion, and I really like the convenience.

One more thing to consider in kitchen lighting. I have under-cabinet lights along the walls in my kitchen, installed under each upper cabinet. But since I have no uppers above my island, I also have no under-cabinet lights there. That's why I chose the three pendant lights for above the island. However, there is no light above my prep sink and it is rather dark and dingy in that part of my kitchen. Since the ceiling is vaulted, it is not an easy fix to hang a light there. The pendant lights hang from a beam just above the island, but there is no beam above my prep sink. Just a warning that you need to think about more than the appearance of whatever light fixtures you pick out.

In your bathrooms, don't forget the "heat-vent-light" combination fixtures. Ours also have a night light feature which I really like. Vanity lights above the mirror are also a must, in my opinion, and sufficient light in the shower. Any more than that is overkill unless you want a chandelier over your spa tub to be really decadent.

Some rooms may not need any ceiling light fixtures at all, depending on your preferences. I personally cannot stand motel rooms that don't have an "overhead" light fixture! They feel so dark and depressing to me, with only lamps to turn on. But if you prefer to have only lamp lighting in a room, you will save on light fixtures and wiring for installation. Just be sure to have at least one light switch that can turn on a lamp from the doorway if you have no ceiling fixture.

In conclusion, from my experience, I would put in a lot fewer lights in the whole house. I would definitely have under-cabinet lighting in the kitchen, and pot lights in most living areas. But if you want a lighted ceiling fan in the bedroom, you don't also need pot lights. If you have pot lights in the living room, you don't also need a center overhead light fixture or chandelier. Think about where you need ambient lighting (like our beam lights facing the ceiling), task lighting (like under-cabinet lights in the kitchen), or pot lights. Remember, too, that lamps are almost always cheaper than installed fixtures and can put the light right where you need it. If I had known then what I know now, I could have eliminated many of our expensive pot lights and light fixtures and cut the electrician's bill in half!

CHAPTER EIGHT

DOORS, WINDOWS, AND FIRE EXITS

You would think that doors and windows would not need their own chapter, but there are many factors to consider when you are designing a home. You must consider energy efficiency, placement and traffic, access to every part of your house, and aesthetics, as well as the general livability of your home. I hope I have remembered all the things I thought of as I was designing my floor plan so you can benefit from some of my ideas and suggestions.

Doors. One of the first decisions I made about all of our doors, interior and exterior, was that they would all have three-foot wide (36") openings. Most standard exterior doors have been 32" and interior doors were 24"– 32" in the recent past, so 36" may or may not be standard with your builder. But just in case either of us were ever in a wheel chair, I decided that our house would be handicapped accessible. I think most wheel chairs would fit through a 32" door, but I was taking no chances. I wanted to be sure there was no problem no matter what the future brought.

Also, I have moved enough furniture in and out of homes that I wanted to be sure any furniture I owned or ever bought would be able to come in through the front door. I also have an old roll-top desk of my grandfather's that will not fit through a regular width door without taking the door off, so problem solved. And the larger door openings make the house seem more spacious in general. I think in most cases, a 32" door will suffice, but this was one area where I wanted extraordinary space, and I'm glad I did. When we moved into our new dream home, the movers were really happy that everything was so easy to move in. No couches or chairs had to be turned on end to fit through any doorways!

I also like pocket doors, and used them in several places to separate different areas of the house. Regular doors that open into a room take up a lot of space in that room when they are open. Especially for any doors that tend to stay open, pocket doors are awesome, as they take up no space on either side of the door, inside or out. I put pocket doors at either end of my walk-in closet so the doors would not stick out into the closet or the adjoining rooms, taking up space. I also used pocket doors for the entrance to the guest suite and the master suite. These doors are usually left open, but can be closed easily when circumstances warrant. Pocket doors are more expensive and have to be put in just right to work properly, but I love having them! "Barn" doors that slide open are also an option, but they do take up wall space when open.

You should consider all options (size, style, cost, materials, etc.) when designing your own doors. They can make a big difference in the overall look of your home as well as noise and temperature control. Double doors on a front entrance or master bedroom, if you have the space and budget for them, can be an awesome feature, too. And don't forget to consider whether you want windows in or beside your front door, so you can see who is at the door. Just remember, if you have windows at your front door, people outside can see you as well, so you may want them partially frosted, tinted or otherwise obscured.

Our builder used solid wood interior doors instead of hollow-core doors. I have no problem with hollow-core doors, but I'm glad now that we went with the solid wood. Solid wood is obviously more expensive, but really adds to the "high-end" quality of the home and insulates noise between rooms much better. Your exterior doors will obviously be solid, whether they are metal, wood, or a composite material. I think our solid wood Knotty Alder front door is the most gorgeous door I've ever seen, and I have received numerous compliments on it from visitors. But you have to shop around to decide what suits your taste and budget best.

I discussed door placement and traffic in chapter two, on layout and design. But don't forget that door placement, in addition to type, size and swing, makes a big difference on space and traffic flow. When you begin to lay out your rooms, the location of every door is key to good planning. Whether it is a door to a hall; into a bedroom, closet or bathroom; or coming in from the garage, you need to think about several factors.

Which way should the door swing? Which side should the hinges be on? Could opening the door interfere with whatever could be happening on the other side of the door? Will a door in this particular location cause a choke point or log jam? If the door is left open, what are the ramifications? Will it be in the way of anything? What will others see through the open door? How will the location of the doors affect the traffic flow in a room? Furniture arrangement? All these things warrant consideration in your design plan.

Let's picture a door coming into the kitchen from the garage. Normally, an exterior door opens into the space it enters. When someone is coming in from the garage, is he going to open the door into someone walking by? Is there a workspace or bathroom near that entrance that may interfere with coming and going? This is what I mean by traffic planning. Also, doorways on either side of a room kind of direct the traffic flow through that room, so you should consider door placement for that reason, as well.

Every door and passageway should be thoughtfully designed. In a bedroom, for instance, no furniture can be placed in the way of the door swinging into the room. If you have another door or closet on that same wall, will there be sufficient wall space for the furniture you want to put in that room? Also, you probably don't want to walk around the bed to get from the door of the bedroom to the bathroom or closet. When you design your rooms, try to picture where you might put certain pieces of furniture in relation to your doorways, closets, and traffic. And be sure you allow clearance for the swing of the door inside or out, unless you plan to use pocket doors. Since I didn't have a good CAD computer program and used regular graph paper, I was easily able to cut out furniture pieces (to scale) and arrange them on paper to be sure everything would fit.

Think of walking into a bathroom and being embarrassed because someone is already in there and didn't lock the door. You will likely excuse yourself and back out sheepishly. The placement of the door in relation to the toilet is a factor to consider, as well as the direction that the door swings. If the door opens away from the toilet, someone coming in may realize the bathroom is already occupied before seeing anything, and back out gracefully. Also, if the door is left open when the room is unoccupied, is the open door along the wall or sticking out in the middle of the room? If you don't consider these things, you may make your space more awkward than it needs to be, and regret your lack of planning down the road.

I tried to put all my doorways either (1) very close to the corner/ wall, or (2) at least two feet from the corner of a room. That way, there would either be no wasted space behind the door, or there would be room for a table or dresser between the door frame and the wall. You should look at each room and doorway critically to see what the best arrangement is, both for inside that room and outside the door, and which way the door should swing when opened. Also remember that there will be trim around each doorway, so allow room for that as well when planning your measurements.

As you get closer to your finished layout, you can get more exacting with your door placement. But the general traffic flow around your house makes general doorway placement important fairly early in your planning. Just try to picture yourself moving about the space to make it most efficient. And your architect/draftsman can help immensely with this if you get stumped.

One last thing about doors. We have dogs and cats at our house, and ever since I bought my first house, I have always built in some sort of cat door or dog door for the critters, and sometimes separate ones for both a dog and cat. We actually built one into the wall at our last house, with a concrete step outside for the critters to land on as they went in or out. My builder thought I was crazy, but that's why it's called "custom" built! Whatever your lifestyle calls for, you can build your house to suit your own needs.

In our current house, I have a back door in the laundry room that leads to a fenced yard on the North side of the house (not visible from the deck or any windows, so doesn't block any views). We built a small back porch with steps down into the yard for the dogs and cats. That makes the laundry room double as a "mud room", as well, which many people find desirable.

This back door has a storm door on it with a built-in dog door in it. That way, when we leave the back door open, the dogs can come and go through the storm door. This is very handy when we are going to be gone from the house a while. Also, if I close the doors to the laundry room, they can get in and out the dog door, but are closed off from the rest of the house if needed. With the dog door built in to the storm door, the house is still fairly well protected from the elements outside. We got the storm door, with the dog door already in it, at our neighborhood hardware store. When the back door is closed, the critters stay either in or out. Very handy, especially when the cats want to bring "critters" in with them, into my house! Lots of possibilities to think about.

Windows. Windows, to me, are the most critical design feature of your home from an aesthetic viewpoint. The number, size, style, color and placement of the windows can make or break your visual appeal, whether from the outside looking in, or inside each room looking out. The quality of the windows can make or break your energy efficiency as well. Remember, though, that the more windows you have, the higher your cost when building. Strategic placement of one window in a bedroom, for instance, may be better than several windows poorly placed. Window size and location must also take fire safety into account. I will discuss fire exits in the next section of this chapter.

Windows not only allow air and light into your home, but allow you to see outside to be a part of the world around you. Do you look out to check the weather? See who is walking or driving by today? The beautiful scenery out your window? The birds at the feeder? The kids at play? The nosy neighbors? And be sure to take into account what others can see of you through your windows. Yes, there are always curtains or blinds, but I like to have my curtains open most of the time to let in the natural light, which also saves electricity. I rarely need to turn on lights in my house during the daytime, as every room has plenty of natural light coming in.

Speaking of natural light, one thing you may not consider when planning your windows is where the sunlight is going to hit inside your house at different times of the day. Will it hit you in the face in the mornings while you are still in bed? Hit a mirror on a wall and bounce off into someone's eyes in the early evenings? Make a prism on a wall? Possibly be a fire hazard if reflected to just the right place? These are admittedly things I observed after the house was built, and I had to plan mirror placement carefully because of some of the sun's angles through some of the windows. But since I did make that observation after the fact, it might help you before hand to consider this factor. Again, an architect would have taken some of that into account, so remember that we are, after all, just novices.

The size, location, and height of your windows can be designed to maximize your looking out and yet minimize what others can see looking in. Take, for example, a bathroom window. If this window is placed at shoulder height, you can still see out when you are standing up, but anyone looking in can only see your head. And if you are sitting down, you still have the sunlight but no one can see you even with the curtains open.

An upstairs bedroom should, in my opinion, have the window sill no lower than waist level. That way, the bed will be below the window level, you can see out, but the angle of anyone looking up and in would only see above the level of your bed or chair, so they really couldn't see much. Also, low windows in an upper level would make me nervous about children falling out an open window.

In a bedroom at ground level, I would put the windows at chest or shoulder height. This would make it safe to walk through the bedroom in any state of undress without the neighbors being able to see, but you can still see out. However, if your neighbor's house is at a higher elevation than yours, this would not apply, and you would want curtains or blinds to prevent them from seeing into your bedroom or bathroom.

Floor to ceiling windows are beautiful, but will be more expensive and may make furniture placement a little more difficult. Think about what furniture and functions you want to put in a room (and where) as you are deciding on window placement and size. The two go hand in hand. And the more windows you have and the bigger they are, the more money you will spend.

Do you want one large window on a wall, two matching windows, or a wall of separate windows? Do you want a window over the kitchen sink? Then where is the kitchen sink going to be? Do you figure out where the sink goes first, or where the window looks best and put the sink there? Just don't forget to consider what each window or group of windows will look like from outside, also. If you want a king size bed on an outside wall, tall narrow windows on either side could be striking. Or a window all across the wall just above the bed's headboard could be beautiful. Be sure to take these ideas into account when designing your windows in every room. It's all up to you!

There are many brands of windows out there, but I say you get what you pay for. I would go with the name brands in most cases, because the quality outweighs any savings you might get from bargain brands. On the other hand, if you shop carefully, you can find quality windows that cost less because the brand doesn't spend as much on advertising. I personally feel you can never have too many windows, but you must have good quality windows to maximize energy efficiency. And there are so many choices, you really should defer to the experts in your area. Visit several different dealers, home improvement stores, etc., and have them tell you why they think their windows are superior. They will all have their own story. Then you take the information and choose whichever source you feel you trust best.

I thought I was really clever, choosing all casement windows with cranks so that the screens were on the inside and would not accumulate spider webs, bugs, etc. Sounded good in theory, but it didn't work. I have screens inside my windows with spider webs in them anyway! I still like the screens inside, though, because they are easier to remove to clean the windows, inside and out, without losing the screens out in the yard! I can do all my window cleaning from inside with casement windows and inside screens.

I also paid extra for the roll screens on the lakeside windows. That way I can roll the screens up and out of sight when the windows are closed and see out more clearly. In my opinion, they are a luxury I could have done without. They are awesome in theory, but really don't make that much difference in everyday use. If I had it to do over again, I would just have regular screens. I seem to leave the roll screens down more than up and away anyway, so really don't use that feature as much as I thought I would. I'm not saying they are bad, just not as awesome for the price as I thought they would be.

Another thing I learned about windows is that one larger window is better than two small windows, and probably cheaper in the long run. In designing my husband's office, I had originally had two windows on either end of the longest wall. For some reason, I decided at the last minute to make one larger window in the middle of that wall instead. I am so glad I did! In a smaller room, with two windows on one wall, there would be little space left for shelves and computer screens that didn't stand in front of the windows! One larger window in the middle of the wall allowed for shelves on either side of the window and a low file cabinet under the window. Much better plan! You really need to think about a lot of different factors to be really happy with your finished product. I'm just glad I figured that one out before it was too late!

Every window you draw in costs more money to build, so plan each one for the most efficient effect. One thing I would do differently is make fewer total windows, with more fixed "picture" windows and smaller operating windows beside or below each one. I don't open even half of the windows I have, and I still have plenty of breeze on nice days when I want to open up. I usually just open one in each room, so I really don't use them all for ventilation. I have several banks of windows with one fixed glass and two casement windows on either side, all the same size. They are gorgeous, but were very expensive. I think if I had it to do over, I might change them into one large fixed picture window with two narrower operating windows on either side for ventilation.

I would have to put some thought into it if I really were to go back to the drawing board, but you can do it now, since you are still in the planning stages. Just be sure you take your time to be sure you will like what you choose. There are lots of options out there for windows. Pictures of homes online or in magazines, showrooms, catalogs and existing homes are good resources for narrowing down your choices.

Fire Exits. Most fire codes require two methods of egress (getting out) from every room in case of fire, especially bedrooms. One exit is obviously the door, but in most cases, the second exit must be a window. In each bedroom, there should be at least one window large enough for a person to exit through it in case of emergency. The type of windows you have will influence how big the opening needs to be in case someone needs to get out through that window. Regular single or double-hung windows would probably be the easiest to open and get out, but I wanted casement windows that cranked open to direct more air inside and allow a better view out. That made it a little harder to imagine escaping through them, but I made them all wide enough to work if it became necessary.

If you have windows that are very far off the ground outside, you might consider having a rope ladder nearby, just in case, to use as a fire escape. Or design a second exit for those rooms so the window doesn't need to be a fire exit. My master bedroom closet is actually a "walk-through" closet to the laundry room, so our second exit is built in to the design. The laundry room has an outside exit (back door) as well, so it would work great as a fire escape if needed. A friend of mine suggested I put an outside entrance there (back door), and I can't imagine it NOT having one now! It was an awesome addition to the general layout.

If you have more than one door to a room, your fire exits are done for you. But be sure to think carefully about traffic, privacy, and furniture arrangement if you have very many doors in a room. It can make a big difference. And the more doors and windows you have, the more you will spend in your overall budget.

CHAPTER NINE

HANDICAPPED ACCESSIBLE?

If you need to make your home handicapped accessible, I would strongly recommend that you obtain a copy of ADA (Americans with Disabilities Act) standards. There are many factors that you probably would not think about, that would need to be addressed to make your home truly accessible.

Our home is not completely accessible, as I did not lower counters or make sinks open underneath cabinets for a wheelchair to roll under. I just made passageways wide enough to easily get around the house if either of us were ever in a wheelchair. One thing I did not take into account, though, was the space around each door for turning a wheel chair into a doorway. In case you want good accessibility, you should do more homework than I did.

Handicapped bars in the bathrooms and ramps instead of stairs are obvious needs, but there are so many other areas that need to be addressed. This chapter is not meant to be a complete list of those factors, just food for thought for long-range planning, if the need should ever arise in your future.

Since we are older, we built our dream home with the possibility of being in a wheelchair someday. Kitchens and bathrooms are particularly critical for accessibility, and I think some thought should be given to doorways and space between cabinets and furniture just in case.... You might even find yourself in a wheelchair short-term after a broken leg or back injury, so the minimum space you might need in order to maneuver around your home should be taken into account.

As I stated earlier, we made our entry doors and all interior doorways 36" wide, just in case one of us might someday be in a wheelchair. This is wider than even the minimum ADA requirements, but I wanted to be sure it would not be a problem. Also, if any of you ever needs one of those little scooter chairs to get around, that will also be easier with wider openings. You may be able to stay in your home longer if you address this possibility in your designs.

In chapter 10 on the kitchen, I mention my custom breadboard at 26" from the floor so I can sit down while chopping veggies, etc. I have arthritis in my back, and standing for any length of time to chop vegetables is painful. Therefore, I had the cabinet maker build me a breadboard beside my cook-top, between two drawers, at just the right height off the floor so I could sit down and chop in comfort. It's great! And I can still see the living room t.v. over the top of the island, even when sitting down! This would be another consideration for handicapped accessibility.

I already mentioned handicapped bars, but I would like to emphasize them again here. I would at least put one outside each shower and beside each toilet and tub, even if you think you will never need them. If you don't want the big long handicapped bars, there are small ones you can put in, in strategic places, to double as towel rods and maybe camouflage that they are actually handicapped bars. That way, if someone accidentally uses them to help themselves stand up in the bathroom, the bars won't pull out of the wall and damage it.

I have a small bar (12") mounted vertically next to my shower entrance that is really not very conspicuous, and I use it regularly when getting in and out of the shower. Bathroom floors can be slippery! Anyone could have an accident in the tub or shower, and it's nice to have grab bars nearby.

If you are going to install grab bars anywhere, though, they should be attached through the wall into a stud so that they will support the weight they need to without pulling out of the wall. Putting wood backing or scrap lumber at certain heights behind the sheet rock, where you know you are going to hang heavy stuff (grab bars, towel bars, mirrors, heavy wall hangings, etc.) is also a good idea. I knew as I was building each room what I intended to put where, so had them add backing in specific places in nearly every room!

One more note about handicapped accessibility. If you are older, or have older family members who will be staying with you from time to time, you need to consider your options on how many stories your house will be. Do you want a basement? Two-story house with the bedrooms upstairs? Even your entries should be considered in the event anyone is injured or in a wheelchair at some point in the future. It is nice to have at least one bedroom downstairs on the main floor for just such an occasion. My dad had a heart attack in his late sixties and the Dr. forbid him from climbing stairs for a couple of months. He had to sleep on a pull-out couch in the living room for that period of time until he could climb stairs again. Obviously, their master bedroom was on the second floor.

Steps up to the front door can obviously present a real problem in this case, so I eliminated that problem from the beginning. We built our retirement home with no stairs at all, except off the back deck. Your building site will determine what your front entry will be like. Stairs and a front porch are visually appealing, but will that present a problem at some point for you or your family? Just food for thought...

CHAPTER TEN

THE KITCHEN

Kitchens and bathrooms are the most expensive rooms per square foot when building a house. They are also the most critical for a comfortable lifestyle and the re-sale value of any home. If the kitchen and bathrooms wow them, buyers can overlook a lot of other drawbacks in a home! I have separated kitchens and bathrooms into two separate chapters because they are each so important.

As you plan your kitchen, you can come up with all kinds of novel ideas to personalize your space. There are nearly infinite ways to lay out your kitchen, and it may be difficult to narrow down your choices. There are also dozens of custom storage options out there for kitchen cabinets, from drawer inserts to lazy susans to swing out mixer stands. This chapter will attempt to break it down and make it a little bit easier to build the design a step at a time.

Kitchen layout options. I wanted a large, open kitchen and designed what I call a "family kitchen". It is all one room with the kitchen on one end and the family room on the other. An oversized island separates the two. That way, I am still a part of whatever is happening in the family room, and can even see the t.v. from my work station in the kitchen. It is an awesome set up and works great for me (see illustration 5 in chapter 2).

There are several types of kitchen layouts. Most common are the galley, L-shape, and U-shape. The galley style kitchen is the most efficient layout. It is made up of two long walls facing each other as if you were in a hallway. Think of a train car with doors on either end and kitchen cabinets on both sides the length of it. This would be a galley style kitchen. The galley kitchen may be the most efficient, but it is usually everyone's least favorite, visually. It can also be crowded if more than one person is using the kitchen at the same time.

Most people today want an open layout with an island of some type. If planned right, the efficient principles of the galley kitchen can be combined with the use of an island, giving you the best of both worlds. Opening up one wall of a galley kitchen by replacing it with an island or peninsula is great. However, you do lose valuable upper cabinets when one side is an island instead of a wall.

My least favorite part about a galley kitchen is the traffic through the "galley", interfering with whatever is going on in the kitchen. A "U" shape prevents this "through traffic" and protects the cook to some extent. I personally prefer either the "L" or "U" shape, with an added island. That way, you have the openness of an island yet have enough of both upper and lower cabinets along the walls to store everything conveniently.

The following illustration shows some different shapes of kitchens: a. galley kitchen, b. L – shaped kitchen, and c. U – shaped kitchen. Any of these can be enlarged to add an island. Or, you can configure your kitchen any way you want. Be creative.

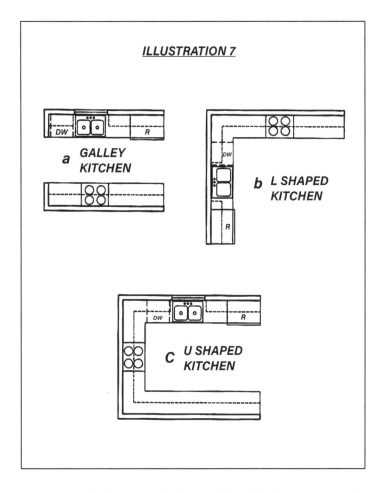

As you are considering your design options, look at your own house or apartment. What do you like or dislike about what you currently have? Notice kitchens at your friends' and relatives' houses and ask them what they like or what they would change about their kitchens if they could. If you know them well enough, look in their cabinets to see how they have their supplies arranged. If you stay alert and observant, you might notice some really cool features at someone else's house that you want to incorporate into yours in some fashion. Whatever your preferences, consider also if you must have a window over your kitchen sink, where your cook top will be in relation to the rest of the kitchen and family space, and if you want an island, peninsula, and/or raised bar. Then you can start playing with possible layouts.

I would also strongly suggest that you visit as many kitchen showrooms as you have time for. Looking at these 3D displays will give you a better idea of what hits your hot button and which layouts will work for you. At this point, you are not looking at the color or style, but the layout and arrangement of the appliances to get ideas. Décor and materials come later, after you design your general layout. You want an efficient and functional kitchen, not just a pretty one! Be sure to take your measuring tape, too, so you can measure layouts you like!

Another source for ideas is real estate open houses. Even if you are not in the market for a ready-made home, you can still attend open houses and see lots of kitchens of every shape, size, and flavor! I know lots of people who do this, and you can especially tour new and higher-end homes to see what the latest trends are.

All these observations will stand you in good stead when you start designing your own space. Floor plan books are great for getting a general feel for layout options, but they are no substitute for an actual 3D kitchen to picture yourself cooking in. And after a while, the floor plans in books begin to look alike. That's why 3D displays in stores or showrooms, or real kitchens in real homes are very helpful. With enough samples to look at, both in books and in person, hopefully it won't take you 25 years to design!

The work triangle. The first thing you should consider when planning your kitchen layout is the "work triangle". This is the triangle formed by measuring from the refrigerator, to the sink, to the stove, and back to the refrigerator. Placement of these three "stations" is crucial to efficient cooking and clean-up. There is obviously a lot more to a kitchen than just this triangle, but let's start with just this one piece of the puzzle. We'll get to the rest later.

The following illustration shows some options for the kitchen work triangle. Kitchen "a" shows an L-shaped kitchen with an island. This work triangle is very efficient, similar to what you might get with a galley layout, but larger and more open. Kitchen "b" shows a U-shaped kitchen with one side as a peninsula. The work triangle here is considerably larger, but still fairly efficient. Kitchen "c" shows a closed galley style with one side open as a peninsula. This one has fewer upper cabinets, but has a large pantry to make up for that.

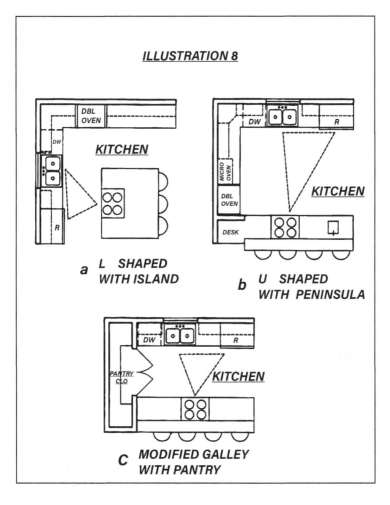

Different sources give varying recommended ranges for the total measurement of the work triangle, but I think common sense dictates what would work best for you. If your work triangle is too small, the kitchen will seem crowded and awkward. If it is too large, you will find yourself running back and forth from place to place, wasting time and energy gathering what you need while you are trying to cook. You want everything you use most often within easy reach as you are preparing meals. Keep that in mind while you are designing your space.

You also want to avoid other features that may block your movement within this triangle. For instance, you would not want a table or an island between the sink and stove that you have to walk around to get from one to the other. You also would not want the refrigerator around the corner or too far away from your work space.

I have seen very expensive and expansive kitchen layouts with the sink on one side of the kitchen and the stove on the other side, with an island in between. This may look very appealing and spacious until you try to prepare a meal in it! Unless you have a team of chefs to do the work for you, this layout is insane! To have an island divide the triangle like that is very inefficient. You want to be able to get from the sink to the refrigerator and stove with as few steps as possible.

I have two sinks in my kitchen: one large main double sink, and a smaller prep sink. The main sink is on the same wall as the refrigerator, and the prep sink is on the island near the cook-top. This leaves the prep sink for food preparation and cooking when the main sink may be full of dirty dishes. I think it is unappetizing to prepare food in the same sink where dirty dishes may be soaking. I can also wash my hands or get a drink of water when someone else is washing dishes at the main sink.

My kitchen's work triangle is approximately 15 feet, measuring from where I stand at all three "stations" of the triangle, using my prep sink instead of the main sink. If I measure using my main sink instead, it is a little larger, at 18 feet. This size works great for me. However, my kitchen is very spacious, because I occasionally have multiple people helping in my kitchen, so it needed to be roomy.

One of our favorite restaurants here at the lake has only one chef, and he purposely has a very tiny triangle in his commercial kitchen. Everything he needs is within reach with only one or two steps taken. I don't know how he can stand it, without getting claustrophobic, but it is extremely efficient since he is the only one using it. He has assistants outside his tiny area do all the other tasks, but he does all the cooking by himself in this one ultra-efficient space. I think his total triangle is 0 feet, maybe just big enough for him to stand in the middle of it, turning to the sides to access all 3 "stations". That obviously would not work for a real kitchen, but it works for him.

I'm not sure that there is a "best" total measurement, and the recommended range varies somewhat from source to source. I saw one floor plan that had a work triangle of 26 total feet, but that would be way too large for any kind of efficiency. I also saw one design with a total of only 6 feet, but I think that would be difficult to work within. I would shoot for somewhere in the 10 to 15 foot range for the total triangle measurement. Much larger than that would not be nearly as efficient.

Keep in mind, too, that the less traffic you have through your kitchen, the better. You don't want people (especially the kids) running in and out of (or through the middle of) your work triangle. Ideally your kitchen should be designed so that the cook is somewhat protected from other activities in the rest of the kitchen. A galley kitchen does not do this, but an island or peninsula may be just the ticket. An "L" could also provide a corner for you to work in, where you won't be jostled by "through traffic". You want to avoid others getting in the way of the cook, or worse yet, bumping into each other as you try to move around the kitchen. That can be very frustrating.

While designing my kitchen, I decided that an island with an "L" shape would provide the right amount of "buffer" between me and any other traffic in the kitchen, since my kitchen allows "through traffic". I put the cook top and a prep sink on the island, with prep space between them, and counter space for slicing and dicing, so I could have two of my three stations in my triangle within easy reach of each other. And no one else passing through the kitchen gets in my way. I have my own little "corner" of the kitchen, with everything I need right there, and am "protected" from other traffic through the rest of the kitchen. And the refrigerator is just across from me there. Others can easily get to the refrigerator, microwave, coffee pot, etc., without passing through my work space. They can also help prep in other parts of the kitchen without affecting my area. It makes for a very efficient layout for me.

Now let's examine each of the three "stations" of the work triangle, starting with the refrigerator. The refrigerator needs to be strategically placed for easy access by the cook, but also to others coming to the kitchen for various reasons. Someone may want to get a drink, fill cups with ice, or help the cook get ingredients out to help get dinner on. Therefore, the refrigerator needs to be near the entrance to the kitchen so others can get to it easily without interfering with whoever is working in the kitchen.

If you design a U shaped kitchen, for example, the refrigerator should be placed at one end of the "U", at the edge of the kitchen, not in the middle of it, so people can easily access the refrigerator without bothering the cook. In the rest of the "U", the cook is somewhat protected because there is no "through traffic" passing through the space. You want others to be able to conveniently access certain areas of the kitchen if they need to, but they should be able to do so without interfering with the main work triangle.

The second station is the sink. In my opinion, the sink should be near the refrigerator, preferably on the same wall, with some counter space and storage between the refrigerator and the sink. That way, it is easy to take foods from the refrigerator and wash or rinse them at the sink before cooking or serving. I also like to put drinking glasses in the upper cabinets between the refrigerator and the sink. That way, you can take a glass out of the cabinet, set it on the counter, and fill it with ice, a cold drink, or water without having to move around any other part of the kitchen. It's all right there together. If you have a prep sink as well, it should be near the stove or cook-top.

The third element of the triangle is the stove or cook-top, and it should be convenient to the sink and refrigerator so you do not waste steps going from one to the other. You will take things from the refrigerator to either the sink or the stove, thus completing the triangle. If you have a cook-top instead of a range, you will have a separate wall oven. For your work triangle purposes, the cook top is the third element in the triangle, not the wall oven.

Preparation and serving space. After you rough in your work triangle, you need to plan the rest of your kitchen. And there is still a lot more to consider! I would start with prep space, to be sure it is convenient to your work triangle. Your preparation/work space is not considered part of the work triangle, but it obviously should be within easy reach of it.

I always seem to prefer slicing and dicing near the cook-top so I can easily put the prepared foods directly into the pan. My cutting board is between the cook top and the refrigerator, which works well for me. You may need more than one prep space, depending on how you use your kitchen. If you bake a lot, you may want a larger prep space near your oven as well. Think about your specific needs, and what kind of space(s) you need.

How many butts does your kitchen need to accommodate? Most kitchens should allow for at least two people to be working in the kitchen at the same time on occasion. My kitchen is designed to accommodate as many as four butts at a time! The primary work triangle is set up for me (or whoever may be the main cook), but there is also a "zone" for clean up at the main sink that does not interfere with my cooking since I have the prep sink handy. Then I have another prep space beside the double ovens and microwave for a third person to work. Finally, if someone needs to get in the refrigerator, they are not interfering with any of the first three. It works great when needed, but my kitchen space may be too big for some people's needs or available space.

While you are planning sufficient prep space, don't forget your serving needs. If you dish all plates up in the kitchen and take them to the table, or if you serve everything at the table, you don't really need serving space in the kitchen. But if you entertain, or ever let your family dish up their own plates, you should plan space for a straight line of counter space, with easy access from both ends, for people to serve themselves. My L-shaped island works great for one person as a prep space, but does not lend itself to serving more than one person at a time. But my raised bar works perfectly for this purpose, on the side without the bar stools. And it is easy to set serving dishes up there from my work space.

Appliances. We have already touched on your refrigerator and stove or cook-top as part of the work triangle. Next on the agenda is all the other appliances you will need in your kitchen, such as the dishwasher, microwave, wall oven(s), and all the small appliances like the coffeemaker, mixer/blender, can opener, toaster, etc. The placement of these should all be planned in relation to the rest of the kitchen layout, and before kitchen cabinets are designed or measured.

Let's start with the dishwasher. It will obviously be next to the sink, but on which side? I have had dishwashers on both the left and right of the sink, and I don't seem to have a preference as to which side works better for me. However, I do have a definite opinion about where it should be in relation to the rest of the kitchen! Be sure to consider where you put the dishwasher in relation to traffic in and through the kitchen. It should be placed so that, when the door is open, it is not in the way of the work triangle or people walking through the kitchen. In our previous family home, my husband and I were constantly dinging our shins on the open dishwasher door when trying to move around in the kitchen!

In our little cabin, which had a galley kitchen, the dishwasher was on the right side of the sink, between the sink and refrigerator. The refrigerator was at the edge of the kitchen, which was very well placed. However, the dishwasher was next in line on the same wall as the sink. When the dishwasher was open, it filled the entire galley space, and no one could get by it to get in or out of the kitchen! If the dishwasher had been on the other side of the sink, away from the refrigerator, we could have at least been able to get to the sink and stove! Very poor planning, whoever designed that kitchen! And the space between the two sides of the galley was only 3 feet, so there was barely room to open the dishwasher to load it.

The following illustration shows two identical kitchens, one with good dishwasher placement, and one with bad dishwasher placement.

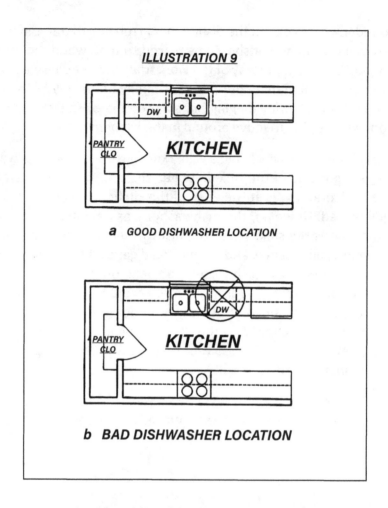

ILLUSTRATION 9

a   GOOD DISHWASHER LOCATION

b   BAD DISHWASHER LOCATION

In my current kitchen, the dishwasher is on the far side of the sink, away from the refrigerator, in a corner of the kitchen that is out of the way of everyone and everything else. If it is open and being loaded, no big deal! I do have to close it to get to the cabinets in that corner, but that is the only time it is in the way. Just take the time to think about these kinds of design and space planning considerations when you are laying out your kitchen.

Next, let's look at the microwave. It can sit on the countertop just fine, but wouldn't you rather have it built in to an upper cabinet so you have less clutter on the countertop? The microwave is another area that other people may want to have access to while you are in the kitchen cooking. Placing the microwave on a separate wall, away from your work triangle, is probably a good idea. Just be sure to allow counter space nearby for setting things on as they go into or come out of the microwave.

Depending on where you put your stove or cook-top, they now make microwaves that double as your stove vent, so the microwave can be mounted directly above your cook top. The vent hood is built into the bottom of these microwaves. This is an awesome feature, but it does make the microwave less accessible to others when you are cooking at the stove. I had this configuration in our last home, but found that steam from pans on the stove fogged over the door of the microwave. This wasn't a big problem, but kind of aggravating. Also, you might need to figure out the best way/direction the door of the microwave should swing to best suit your layout.

Now to the wall oven(s). I chose a stainless steel (gas) cook top for my island instead of a complete range in that location. Since I had no uppers above the island cook-top, I needed all the storage space under the cook-top that I could get. The other reason I chose this configuration was that I wanted double ovens! I put the double ovens on another wall, away from my work triangle. By the way, I strongly recommend this layout if your space and budget allow for that option. I LOVE my double ovens (both full-sized ovens, one above the other), and it is surprising how often I use them both in the same meal. I don't know how I did without them for big family gatherings at Thanksgiving and other holidays! I prefer a gas cook-top, but an electric oven for carbon monoxide considerations. A hood vent above, or a down-drafting vent (under the floor) are also options to consider.

Again, whatever suits your preference is best, as long as you do your homework and know what you want. If you are a gourmet or really enjoy cooking and entertaining, you may even want to choose a large commercial-style range with lots of bells and whistles. However, you will also pay a premium for all those extras!

Small appliances are next, and you may have a ton of them! They can clutter a nice countertop quickly. I built in two appliance garages to de-clutter the countertop, but the two garages actually take up too much of my wonderful countertop space! I wish I had made my corner appliance garage larger, and just made one of them. But at least I can get my toaster, coffee maker, blender, crock pot, popcorn popper, etc. out of sight but still very handy.

I put electrical outlets and under-counter lighting in my appliance garages, so I can just slide out the toaster, for instance, use it and slide it back out of sight with very little effort. The appliances in the garage can stay plugged in if I want them to, and it is so easy to slide them out and use them without having to mess with plugging them in. I love this feature and am pleased that someone invented the concept of the appliance garage!

If you don't want to build in an appliance garage, at least consider where you will store all of your small appliances so they will be fairly easy to get to. I have some of my rarely-used ones on the top shelf of my pantry. I can still get to them, but they are out of the way and not cluttering my countertop. My can opener is one small appliance that I have out on the countertop, because it needs to be near my cook-top and prep space. I had it in one of the appliance garages, but that necessitated me travelling across the kitchen every time I needed to open a can when cooking. It makes more sense to be out on the island where I use it.

Kitchen storage. Before you solidify your work triangle, you must consider storage around each of the 3 stations, as well as the rest of the kitchen, for the supplies you will need for each area. No matter how efficient your work triangle is, if you do not have sufficient storage near each station, that efficiency goes right out the window. It is very important to consider what storage needs go along with each part of your kitchen, especially in the work triangle. You must plan your storage areas relative to where you would most logically use items when you are planning your kitchen layout and storage space.

You will also want to plan which cabinets will contain which "like items". For example, if the coffee pot is in a corner appliance garage (hopefully near a sink for easy filling), then the coffee and filters, supplies, cups, etc., can go in the uppers above the appliance garage so everything related to coffee is all right there handy. Wherever your microwave is, you can store all the microwaveable containers, accessories, etc., in the uppers just above the microwave. Spices for cooking obviously need to be convenient to the cook-top, etc. Just go through your daily routines in your mind and you can come up with some super-cool solutions for arranging your kitchen and supplies specifically to your liking. This is what customized design is all about!

Back to storage at your three work stations. Let's start with the stove or cook-top. It probably needs the most storage space. If your stove is in an island or peninsula, you may not have any upper cabinets to store all the things you will need close at hand while cooking. Herbs and spices, seasonings, cooking oil, flour and sugar canisters, can opener, pots and pans, cooking utensils, knives, and all other frequently-used items and ingredients all need to be located at your cooking station. This all takes quite a bit of storage where there may be only lower cabinets and drawers.

There are lots of special drawers, bins and pull-out shelves available with most cabinet lines in which to store these things. But I really miss being able to keep my spices and other cooking ingredients above the stove and my pots and pans below. If your cook-top is not on the island, you will have upper cabinets to help with storage right above your cook space. But I wanted my cook-top on the island so I was more a part of the family while I was preparing meals. I finally found room near my cook-top for everything I use most often, but it was not easy. Thank heavens for lazy susans in corner cabinets! The newer ones are so easy to use and give you lots of extra storage space.

One thing I like in newer cabinet designs is the long, deep drawers for your lower cabinets (instead of shelves behind doors) to keep cookware and other supplies in. If you have not seen these, they are 8" to 12" deep and 30" to 36" wide. They can hold mixing bowls, bakeware, pots and pans, etc. These are great, and you can see everything you have without having to bend over or get on the floor to get at what you need out from under your cabinets. You can also get the slide-out shelves for your lowers that are in place of the lower shelves, but I like the newer big drawers better. What a great solution to the dark, awkward space under your counters!

One more thing about the cook-top, before I move on. Since mine is on the island, I don't have a vent hood above it. Instead, I put an under-counter venting system in behind the cook-top, which vents the smoke and smells out under the house to the back yard. This is pretty expensive, and may necessitate you putting your cook-top on a wall with a regular hood vent. Again, just food for thought.

Once you figure out where your cooking supplies, relative to your stove or cook-top, will take up residence, the next item is dishes and tableware. My personal opinion is that all dishes, glassware, and tableware should be near the refrigerator, sink and dishwasher. This is where you would pour drinks, use them to serve food out of the refrigerator, and where you put them away when you empty the dishwasher. I can't imagine where else you would store these items! It would be nice if these cabinets were also close to where you would use them to set the table, but I personally feel it is more important to have them near the refrigerator, sink and dishwasher.

106

My cups and glasses are stored in the upper cabinets, between my refrigerator and sink. The plates, bowls and serving pieces are on the other side of the sink, above the dishwasher. The silverware and table ware is in a drawer next to the refrigerator, below the glasses cabinet. That way, everything is easy to put away when you empty the dishwasher. Dishcloths and kitchen towels are in the next drawer down, under the silverware, because that is where I use them – next to the sink!

Regardless of where you put your refrigerator, be sure that there is adequate counter space beside it. There must be space beside the refrigerator in order to conveniently set items down as they go into or come out of the refrigerator. You also need to plan adequate countertop space on both sides of the sink for work space and dirty dishes.

Next comes the oven(s). You naturally will want all your bakeware, cookie sheets and pot holders near your oven. I also keep all my mixing bowls there, even though I may use them at my cook-top as well. It just makes sense to store things where they will be used most. And again, be sure and plan counter space beside your oven, to set items on as they go into or come out of the oven.

The pantry may be set off a bit from your work triangle, especially if it is very large. But if your most frequently-used items are near your work space, other lesser-used items can go in the pantry, such as boxed and canned goods. One trip to the pantry to get out main ingredients for a particular meal is no big deal, as long as all the most-used items are near your work space.

I also like to keep my kitchen cleaning supplies in the kitchen, either under or over the sink. When our kids were little, I moved all the cleaning supplies up over the sink instead of under it, to help "kid-proof" the house. I liked it so well that way that I still keep them above the sink. They are much easier to see and reach, and

I keep pitchers, trash bags, etc., under the sink. However, I keep ONLY my kitchen cleaning supplies in the kitchen.

I keep all my bathroom cleaning supplies in each of my bathrooms, under the sink. What a novel idea, if I do say so myself! That way, I don't have to haul cleaning supplies all over the house. I keep all my other cleaning supplies (rags, floor cleaners, dusters, glass cleaner, carpet shampoo, etc.) in a special "cleaning closet" with my brooms, vacuum cleaner and bags, etc. I did not have this luxury in our previous house, and am delighted with how nice it is to have all this custom storage and organizational space! It makes every activity of daily living so much easier, and everything has its place so you can actually find what you are looking for!

Custom cabinets & countertops. Now for the cabinets, countertops, and appliances. I would start with the cabinets and their wood choice, quantity, style, color, and stain, then the sinks and countertops. Finally, I would choose the appliances. You must decide on exactly what appliances you are going to put in, and their exact size, before you finalize your cabinet and countertop plans. Do you want a compact cook-top or a large commercial-sized range? Do you prefer a side-by-side refrigerator/freezer? French style doors? How large will your kitchen sink be? You can pick out your style and color on your cabinets and countertops, but you cannot finalize your measurements until you pick out all of your appliances.

Your wood choice for cabinets varies from oak (my least favorite but one of the most inexpensive), to cherry, maple, etc. All have their distinctive grains and color choices. My cabinetry throughout the whole house is made of Knotty Alder with a dark stain, but I love rich dark wood and a more rustic look. Some people may prefer light wood, painted surfaces, metal or glass. There are lots of options, so do your homework to see what pleases you most.

The styles of doors and drawer fronts are also numerous. After you choose the wood, style and color, you have to choose the hardware that goes on them. Drawer and door pulls are an important choice for whatever look you are going for. Once you arrive at a style you like, look at lots of different stores and vendors to compare prices. Again, the most expensive may not necessarily be the best, and the cheapest may not be the worst.

While you are looking at cabinet choices, be sure to check out all the storage options. There are spice drawer inserts, drawer dividers, lazy susans for corner cabinets, pull-out shelves for under-counter cabinets, and large deep drawers for cookware instead of under-counter shelves (a MUST for my kitchen). If I had it to do over again, I might not have ANY shelves under my cabinets – they would all be the large deep drawers! I absolutely love mine! In our old house before we remodeled the kitchen, I can remember having to get down on the floor in the kitchen to get to cookware in the lower shelves that were behind other items. Not any more! Between the pull-out shelves and the giant drawers in newer kitchens, that problem is solved!

I also have a swing-out mixer stand for my electric mixer that stores under the counter behind a door, and then swings out and up and locks in place for me to use my mixer right there on the stand! It is the one most awesome feature in my kitchen! I didn't use my mixer that much before, so it was always stored in a high cabinet above the oven or refrigerator and I had to get a step stool to get it down, then lift it way back up there to put it away! I use it much more now because it is so handy!

And don't forget the under-counter double pull-out trash cans! We use one for regular trash and the other for recycle trash. It is so convenient, and no trash cans sitting around for the dogs to get into!

I built in a custom "bread board" at exactly 26" off the floor. It pulls out from between two drawers so that I can sit down in a regular chair and chop veggies near the stove. Bread boards are usually built in above a bank of drawers, to slide out from under the counter top. But I wanted mine at chair height so I could sit down to do most of my prep and chopping before I actually start cooking. So mine is under the first drawer instead of above it. I cannot stand for long periods without my back hurting, so if I can sit down for most of my chopping and prepping, then I can stand while I actually cook.

I sit and chop my onions, veggies, etc., even while watching the t.v. over the fireplace on the other side of the family room. Then, when the chopping is done, I can just toss them in the pan and start cooking. My custom designed "bread board" is a life saver for me. I use a vinyl cutting sheet on the wood bread board surface to protect it and keep it clean. Then the cutting sheet can go right into the dishwasher when I'm done chopping! I wipe off the bread board and shove it back in, and it is ready for next time. I also use it to hold a cookie sheet so I can sit down while I am dropping cookies on it or spreading pizza dough, etc. It works great!

After you choose your cabinetry and all the bells and whistles you want with them, you need to choose your countertops and sinks. I know granite countertops have been the popular choice for several years now, but it does have its drawbacks, in addition to its price. Talk to different countertop dealers who carry many different types and brands of countertops to get a better comparison on prices, pros and cons of each type. Some stain more easily than others, and some solid surface materials can scorch or crack if you put a hot pan on them. Some need to be sealed repeatedly over the life of the material, while others may chip or crack.

Concrete countertops are another popular up-and-coming material gaining in popularity. However, concrete needs to be well sealed and kept sealed to keep out moisture and bacteria, as does granite. And don't overlook the newer laminate countertops if you are on a tight budget. They are inexpensive, durable, and can look very much like granite! Just do your homework and decide which cabinets and materials/designs work best for you. That way, there are no unpleasant surprises when the cabinets go in! And ask around for reputable installers, if your builder doesn't have a favorite crew to install your countertop.

Be sure you research different types of materials before choosing your kitchen sinks, too. Our countertops are solid surface with seamless attached sinks of the same material. Our solid surface countertops and sinks don't stain and are easy to clean. I love them! Some people like stainless steel sinks in their kitchen, but unless you polish them after every use, I think they look dirty and show every water spot. And porcelain can chip or wear down to the supporting cast iron over time.

Our builder used a cabinet maker (instead of commercial cabinets available at home improvement stores) for all our cabinets, trim, and closets. Commercially available cabinets are probably less expensive, but not always. Your builder will usually recommend the type of cabinets he/she is used to working with, but comparison shopping never hurts. I absolutely love my custom cabinets, but we did go way over budget by choosing the number and quality of cabinets that we did.

ESK (Eating Space in the Kitchen). One more thing before we move on. I have a formal dining room, and a bar with bar stools in my kitchen. I did have a "nook" off to the side of the kitchen designed for my kitchen table, but took most of that space to make a ½ bath instead. I am really sorry I did that. I could have put the ½ bath somewhere else and kept my breakfast "nook". My kitchen table is now out on the covered deck, which is right off the kitchen, but I do not have any real eating space in the kitchen except the bar. I think every kitchen should have space for at least a small kitchen table. Just sayin'...

Common measurements. For ease in drawing your rough kitchen layout, the following measurements may be helpful.

However, you MUST measure exact appliance sizes and get specs on your model numbers for your builder and cabinet maker before finalizing your plans.

1.) Plan on your refrigerator taking up approximately 3 feet in width, and approximately 32" in depth.

2.) A standard dishwasher is approximately 24" across.

3.) Your cook-top or range may be from 24" to 36" wide, depending on what you choose.

4.) A standard kitchen cabinet is 24" deep, and the countertop will have about a 1" overhang beyond the edge of the cabinets.

5.) Your kitchen sink will vary, depending on the type you choose, but generally will range from 24" to 36" for a double sink. A prep sink of 16" is very adequate.

6.) A nice-sized microwave is 24" wide.

7.) A standard wall oven is approximately 30" wide.

8.) 18 to 24" is large enough for a standard cutting board and adequate prep space for slicing and dicing. More width would probably be needed for baking.

9.) You should allow a minimum of 4' between countertops, but 5' would be better.

10.) Standard countertop height = 36", table height = 28 to 30", raised bar=42".

CHAPTER ELEVEN

BATHROOMS AND LAUNDRY

This chapter was going to be only about bathrooms. I decided to add the laundry room here because it just seemed to fit. Besides, some people actually put their laundry area in a bathroom, or a toilet and shower in their laundry room, so it seemed appropriate to combine the two into one chapter.

Bathrooms. Bathrooms are the next biggest investment in your entire house, and their cost per square foot is second only to the kitchen. In my opinion, every home needs at least two bathrooms, even if one is only a half bath. There are just times when one can't wait for someone else to get out of the bathroom! The more bathrooms you have, the better the resale value of your home, also. We have two full baths and one half bath. I think, for most homes, that is a sufficient number. However, if you have two or more floors in your house, you will want at least one bathroom on each level.

I would definitely put a spacious bathroom, with a separate shower and a garden type bathtub, in the master suite. Unless your budget just won't allow it, this en suite bathroom will greatly enhance your lifestyle and the re-sale value of your home. Another full bath should be near the rest of the bedrooms, but could just have a shower or bath/shower combo instead of the separate shower and tub.

Bathrooms are expensive to build, but nearly impossible to add (cost effectively) after the home is built, so I would design in an adequate number of them to meet your needs from the beginning.

In addition to your master bedroom en suite bathroom and a full second bathroom, I strongly suggest a half bath somewhere near the living and/or family room area. A bathroom right off the kitchen is not too appealing, but it could be right around a corner. The half bath near the living areas is nice and convenient for guests to use without seeing the more private areas of your home. It is also wise to place the half bath near the kitchen to capitalize on the water and sewer lines already running to the kitchen.

Some homes have 3, 4, 5, or more bathrooms, but that to me is an overkill unless you have a huge house with numerous floors and lots of kids. Why spend the money? I think 2 ½ baths should be sufficient for most homes, but that is just my personal opinion. One caviat, however: there should be at least a half bath on every floor. If you have a two story house with a basement, you should obviously have a full bath on each floor that has a bedroom on it, and at least a half bath on any other floors in the house.

A mud room with a toilet and shower in it, opening to the back yard, is also a nice feature that is fairly popular. This could be designed in combination with the laundry room, if that is a configuration you would use. Again, it all depends on your lifestyle, personal needs, budget and priorities.

Bathtubs. Regardless of how many bathrooms you have, you should have at least one bathtub. Even if is just to bathe the dog, every house needs at least one tub! But if that one is in the master bathroom, I'm warning you now that everyone will want to borrow it, and there goes your private bathroom!

I have a thing about cast iron tubs, too. Acrylic or fiberglass may be much less expensive, but a cast iron bathtub will probably outlive you, your children, and your grandchildren! Both bathtubs in my house are ceramic over cast iron, and I am so glad I went with those. If you keep them clean and don't scratch them with harsh abrasive cleansers or steel wool, they will look new for nearly forever. Nearly any cleaner and hot water will shine them up nicely without much elbow grease. And they won't stain unless the surface gets scratched. Again, cast iron tubs are much more expensive than fiberglass or acrylic, but I feel the extra cost is worth it long term.

Showers. As far as showers go, a large shower in the master suite is very nice. And the walk-in showers are extra nice! Our master bathroom shower is a little bit of an overkill, at 5' X 5'! But I would not make a shower any less than 3' X 3', as an inside measurement.

For your shower surround, I would suggest using ceramic tile or cultured marble. Fiberglass or acrylic inserts are much less expensive, but they do not hold up long term. They also become difficult to clean when they get some age on them. All the acrylic inserts I have seen are just too small for my tastes as well. Again, it all depends on your space and budget. There may be newer materials now that will hold up better, but I personally prefer the old tried and true ceramic tile in a shower. We used cultured marble panels on our walls and ceramic tile on the shower floor. This seems to have been a good choice, and seems to be easy to clean and is holding up well so far.

Sinks. If you have the space and budget, double sinks are a must in my opinion, especially for the master bath. I have my double sinks outside the bathroom itself for brushing teeth, shaving, make-up, etc., so that the actual bathroom is saved for what it's supposed to be used for! I also have a small sink inside the bathroom, just for washing hands. Some people may think that is extravagant (3 sinks for one bathroom), but I want to wash my hands after using the toilet, not open the door and use the sink outside the bathroom. Again, just my own personal preference. The double sinks outside the master bath are kind of an 80's style feature, but I like mine a lot.

We also built our guest bath with a similar configuration as the master, putting double sinks in a separate area just outside the bathroom. That way, when a bunch of the kids' friends are here, or all the kids descend on us at once, one or two can be using the outer sink area while another is taking a shower or using the restroom in the separate bathroom area. Between the two of us, we have 6 kids (four of them girls!), 10 grandkids, and 5 great-grandkids, so we knew bathroom space and efficiency would be an important consideration in our dream home. Our set-up works well, especially if everyone is getting ready to go somewhere at the same time! Also, if you have girls (especially teen-agers), be prepared to need extra bathroom and vanity space!

Bathroom and linen storage. While I am on the subject of the guest bath, I want to comment on a custom storage solution I came up with, based on a friend's idea. In our previous house, the kids' bathroom sink area was always cluttered with lots of grooming aids such as blow dryers, curling irons, razors and toiletries. I therefore built in a custom storage space between the two sinks, in both the guest bathroom and the master bath. I also have a bank of regular drawers under the countertop between the two sinks, and the usual storage space under each sink.

My custom solution, which our cabinet maker built specifically to my specs, is a built-in cabinet that sits on the vanity countertop between the two sinks. It is 12" wide by 40" tall by 8" deep (all inside measurements), with adjustable shelves. These cabinets can be recessed into the wall as well, but I didn't think to do that. I wish I had, as it would have taken up less space on the vanity in both bathrooms.

These cabinets provide ample storage for toiletries, as well as the above-mentioned grooming aids and appliances. What makes them unique, though, is that the cabinets have electrical outlets wired right inside them, much like my appliance garages in the kitchen.

Getting the curling irons, etc., off the countertops does three things. It reduces the clutter, places them in a convenient location, and increases safety as well. When used as intended, we don't have cords dangling off the counter or across the sink while using them. They are plugged in inside the cabinet where they are away from water sources. And, they are less likely to get knocked off into the sink or onto the floor, which can be a hazard. When you are done using a grooming appliance, you simply turn it off, let it cool off, and shove it back into the cabinet, still plugged in. That way it is out of sight when not being used, and I love it! Now if I could just get the kids to actually USE the storage I so painstakingly designed for them!!

I strongly recommend that you allow storage space for linens and towels in the bathroom as well. There is nothing worse than getting out of the shower and realizing that you forgot to bring a clean towel in with you! If the linen cabinet is in the bathroom, no problem! And be sure to plan plenty of convenient towel rods for face towels, wash cloths, and bath towels, all readily available where you will need them.

Accessories. I put double towel rods outside the tubs and showers in my house to make sure everyone had space to hang their towels close to the shower. I also put a handicapped bar in place of a towel rod over my garden tub in the master bath, and on the wall in my half bath so it would be safe for someone to grab onto them if need be. I put two handicapped bars in my shower, also, for steadying myself in the shower when needed and for hanging wash cloths and loofahs on.

My mom used to try to use our towel bars to steady herself in the bathroom, and I was always afraid they would pull out of the wall and she would fall. So I put scrap pieces of wood in as backing behind my sheet rock in strategic areas so all my towel rods would be attached to more solid supports than just sheet rock. I also put small handicapped bars in place of towel rods in strategic places for support, also attached to either a wood backing or a stud behind the wall.

Dimensions and design. Floor plan books are great sources for bathroom layouts. It's amazing how small and efficient you can make a full bathroom and save lots of space and money. A nice, traditional 3-piece bathroom can be built in approximately 5' by 7'. However, the larger the bathroom(s), the more luxurious you feel when using them.

The following illustration shows three possible bathroom layouts: small, medium, and large. It also shows my own bathroom layout with the walk-through closet adjacent.

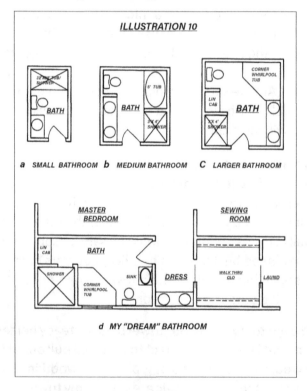

ILLUSTRATION 10

a SMALL BATHROOM   b MEDIUM BATHROOM   C LARGER BATHROOM

d MY "DREAM" BATHROOM

When you are out and about, at stores, friends' homes, etc., make a note of different bathroom layouts. Then, when you are ready to design your own, you will have a good handle on what you want. One caution: be sure to allow at least three feet in front of the toilet to sit down and stand up. Any less than that might make you feel crowded or claustrophobic. More than three feet is preferable, but at least three feet should be the minimum. I also like to leave a little space between the toilet and the vanity or wall so I have room for a trash can, extra toilet paper, the bowl brush, and plenty of elbow room.

Another suggestion is to arrange the toilet and vanity in such a way that you can reach the space under the sink for spare toilet paper, sanitary products, etc., while sitting on the toilet. Or, if that doesn't work for your space, leave room beside the toilet for a small free-standing shelf or cabinet to hold those items.

While you are designing your bathroom layout, the following dimensions should be helpful:

1.) Most standard bathtubs are 24" to 30" wide by 5' long.

2.) Most vanity tops are 24" deep. They can be as narrow as 18", but I would not make one smaller than 24". Standard vanity height is 32".

3.) A double sink vanity cannot fit in less than 5', but I would make mine no shorter than 6'. Just more elbow room.

4.) A standard toilet should be centered in no less than a 3 foot space.

5.) A shower should be no smaller than 3' square.

6.) A linen cabinet does not need to be deeper than 10", but more is roomier.

7.) Spa tubs may be longer and wider than standard tubs. Be sure and measure.

JAN JONES EVANS

Laundry room. The laundry room in my dream home is perfect for me. It is between my master bedroom closet, my sewing room, and my guest suite. Most older homes have the laundry area in the basement, next to (or in) the garage, or even IN the kitchen! How dumb is this? For one thing, you want your laundry room nearer your bedrooms and bathrooms, where most laundry is generated and put away. And your utilities (furnace, water heater, etc.) need to be more centrally located to be most efficient. So I put my laundry room in the bedroom wing and the furnace, etc., near the center of the house.

I knew I wanted the laundry room close to the bedrooms, but even so, I originally had it just inside the garage, where I now have my husband's office/"man cave". The reason I originally put the laundry/utility room by the garage entrance is because that's where it was in our previous house. But when I was choosing which rooms would have the beautiful lake view, I realized that the laundry room did not need a view! That's when I figured out to put the office there. Once I had made that decision, I started playing with where to put the laundry room. That's when I came up with its current location, which is awesome.

Most of your laundry is generated in and near the bedrooms and bathrooms, so why not arrange the laundry room in a centrally located place amongst the bedrooms, where most of your clothes and linens are dirtied and then put away after washing? Seems like a no-brainer to me! Many newer homes have this feature now, but older homes sure don't! Just seems like something you would want to design into your floor plan to be much more efficient and convenient. That way, you aren't carting laundry baskets all over the house, up and down stairs, and the like.

When choosing the location of the laundry room, don't forget that the dryer must go on or very near an outside wall, to easily vent it to the outside. My laundry room also has an outside entrance leading in from the back yard, so it can double as a mud room and fire escape route. I did not originally have this door in the design, but my best friend suggested it, and now I can't imagine how I would have done without it!

My laundry room also has several custom features I designed to make everything more organized. I wanted to have plenty of space IN the laundry room for all the laundry baskets in all the various stages of getting the laundry done [baskets of: (1) dirty clothes, (2) clean clothes to be folded, and (3) clean clothes that are sorted and folded and ready to be put away]. I don't like laundry cluttering up my living areas while I am working on folding or sorting it (in case someone drops by), but it still happens sometimes anyway.

Our house in Oklahoma had a large laundry room with a nice counter top for baskets and sorting. Even with that, I still had a problem keeping up with it. When we added on to the back of the house, we needed to close off the back door in the laundry room. Closing in this door gave me additional space in the laundry room, so I had to decide what to put there instead. I had my builder build me a custom laundry sorting cabinet, which I probably should have patented. I'm not sure how you would go about patenting something like that, so I never bothered. But it is an awesome solution to dirty laundry accumulating, especially for large families!

My custom laundry sorting cabinet is a built-in cabinet that is 3 feet wide, 2 feet deep, and 6 feet tall, with storage on top as well. It has adjustable shelves, and I use it for storing 8 laundry baskets (two on each shelf). Each basket is labeled for sorting dirty laundry into categories for washing (colors, whites, underwear, delicates, towels, etc.).

When a hamper is full in a bathroom or bedroom, you take it into the laundry room and sort it into the correct basket. Whatever your sorting technique is, you just label the baskets the way you would normally sort your laundry. Then, when a given basket is full, you slide it out, wash that load, and slide it back in to accumulate more dirty laundry! It actually works the way I intended it to work, and it is absolutely awesome! I keep extra baskets on top of the washer to put clean clothes into when they come out of the dryer. I use these to sort/fold and put away the clean laundry.

I had our builder here make the exact same cabinet in my new laundry room, and I absolutely love it! I don't know how I did without it before. Laundry used to be such a project, and there was no place to sort it for washing! And we only had three kids! I don't know what families do with even more children! It is now so much easier to do, I think everyone should have one!

In theory, there are never any overflowing hampers or laundry baskets in the whole house – ever! That is, if you actually DO the laundry often enough to keep up with it! My husband would argue that I don't consistently do a good job of that! Well, he could help, ya know! Actually, he has been known to wash socks or darks, for instance, if he is running low. Bless his little heart!

My laundry room is at the other end of my walk-through master closet. Again, the theory to this design was so that I can take clothes out of the dryer and immediately hang them up right there in my closet. Wonderful design feature, but sometimes the best laid plans.... I usually prefer to sit down on my bed or in the living room in front of the t.v. to sort and fold laundry. But at least I do have room in the laundry room to put it if someone does drop by! I know some people who use their dining room table for sorting and folding their clean laundry. That's fine, if you have no other choice, but wouldn't it be better to build a sorting table into your laundry room?

Some features you may want to consider for your laundry room design include:

1.) plenty of storage for all the laundry items you use (detergent, bleach, etc.)

2.) a table or counter of some sort for sorting and folding the clean laundry (similar to what you use at a laundromat)

3.) a laundry sink for hand washing, rinsing, pre-treating, soaking or drip drying

4.) a clothes bar above the laundry sink for hanging wet clothes that cannot be dried in the dryer

5.) a bar above the washer and dryer (or other area) for hanging clean clothes until you get around to taking them to the room in which they belong

6.) an ironing board in or around the laundry room

7.) a laundry basket cabinet for sorting dirty clothes like I described above

I mentioned that I have an exterior door in my new laundry room, coming in from the back yard. This allows for several things. The laundry room can double as a "mud room", what with the deep laundry sink in there. I did not put a toilet or shower there, because that was not an important feature for us. But for some families, depending on their hobbies, yard work, etc., it would be a great feature to add.

The back door in the laundry room also doubles as an alternative fire exit from the bedrooms, since it is centrally located to all of them (see Chapter 6 in the section on fire exits). By putting a back entrance in the laundry room, I was also able to add a dog door to the back yard. The dog door is built into the storm door so it is easy to open or close, depending on our needs. The dog door in that location led to the idea of fencing the area on the North side of the house that did not block our view of the lake from our deck. It all fell into place wonderfully when all was said and done.

For years after permanent press came along, I did very little ironing. I still do very little, but since I have time to sew now, I use my iron and ironing board more. My mom taught me that ironing between steps makes sewing much easier! So I built in one of those shelves that hold both the iron and the ironing board on the wall just outside the laundry room, in a corner of the sewing room. That way it is convenient to both rooms but out of the way. And I made sure to put it near an outlet for plugging in the iron.

Thinking of all these organizational, storage, and personal solutions can really make your home a "dream" to live in! I am so thankful that I had all those years to think about and come up with all these types of ideas and solutions!

CHAPTER TWELVE

STORAGE, CLOSETS, AND CABINETS

I don't care how much of a cliché it is, YOU CAN NEVER HAVE TOO MUCH STORAGE! Knowing this, I went WAY over budget with all the cabinets and storage I built into this house. But that is also what makes it a custom-built house! Quality built-ins were a high priority feature for me, and I use every square inch of cabinets in every room. It is so awesome to have a place for everything, and everything in its place! Organization is a real stress-buster for me, and greatly enhances my quality of life. This chapter will deal with all the options for built-ins you may want to include in your designs, from book shelves to storage or china cabinets to closets. Remember, built-ins are expensive, but they also may define the "custom" in your home.

Kitchen cabinets. Your kitchen cabinets will be one of your biggest budget items, but are also one of the most important considerations in your home design. The kitchen needs to be the most functional design of nearly anything else in your house, and will be the most-used room in most homes. In today's family, the kitchen is often the hub of the household. Be sure and put lots of thought into your kitchen design. You will be glad you did!

I devoted an entire chapter to the kitchen in Chapter 10, so I do not feel that I need to cover much detail here. However, adequate storage for, and convenient access to, all the things that you will use in your kitchen are key to a successful design. Once your work triangle and layout are determined, you need to consider storage for each category of "stuff" you will need to find room for in your kitchen. From cookware to dishes, food, spices and cooking utensils, all your storage needs to be planned out for maximum efficiency.

Standard kitchen base cabinets are 24" deep and 36" high off the floor. Upper cabinets are generally 12" deep. Your measurements may vary slightly, depending on your cabinet maker. Be sure to allow enough space between your cabinets and island, if you have one, for moving around easily. I would not design less than 4 feet between cabinets, and more if possible, depending on your layout. And don't forget to consider the space needed to open doors, refrigerator, oven, dishwasher, etc. while you are working in the kitchen, and plan accordingly.

Kitchen pantry. Every kitchen should have a pantry, no matter what size. My pantry is huge, but wouldn't have needed to be so big. It is right around the corner from my refrigerator, slightly outside the kitchen proper. If you can fit yours in the main part of the kitchen, great. But it doesn't have to take up valuable space there. The things you will store in your pantry are not like the spices and ingredients you will use right at the stove for nearly every meal. You will most likely store your canned and boxed goods, as well as maybe paper goods and other less-frequently used items in the pantry. Therefore, the pantry should be near the kitchen, but doesn't have to be as accessible as other kitchen storage. Please refer back to the section on kitchen storage in Chapter 10.

My pantry is very large, at 5 feet wide by 28 inches deep (inside measurements). It goes from the floor up to regular ceiling height at 8 feet. It has double doors that are 2 feet wide each (four foot total opening), and 6'9" tall, making it very easy to see and reach all contents. My pantry is very deep, but the shelves inside are only 16" deep, with wrap-around shelves on the sides that are 6 inches deep. This configuration makes it almost a "walk-in" pantry. It also leaves room for wire shelves to be mounted on the inside of the pantry doors, which is very handy. By the shelves being recessed, also, I can reach and utilize the storage space on shelves all the way to the ceiling.

I designed my pantry shelves to accommodate larger dog and cat food sacks, kitty litter, cases of water bottles, etc., on the floor under the first shelf. Therefore, I made the first shelf start at 24" off the floor. The rest of the shelves (4 total) are 16" apart, which accommodates everything I need to store on them (tall cereal boxes, saltine cracker boxes, 2 liter soda bottles, standing paper towel rolls, lesser-used small appliances, etc.). I even have room for all my cookbooks and recipe boxes on the top shelf!

I love my pantry, but it may be too large for most house plans, especially as deep as mine is. If you have the space and money, the bigger the better. But for most people, I think 3 to 4 feet wide by 12" deep would be sufficient for food storage. A larger pantry or other separate storage space for additional items like light bulbs, paper goods, cleaning supplies, etc., is also helpful. Just be sure to think about all the items you need to store and plan your pantry or other storage space(s) accordingly.

Broom closet. You may want to design a closet near the kitchen or laundry room specifically for mops, brooms, and cleaning supplies. I have a really large cleaning closet where I put all my cleaning supplies. It is so convenient to have it all together (mops, brooms, vacuum, rags, vacuum cleaner bags and accessories, carpet shampoo, glass cleaner, dusting supplies, spray cleaners, etc.) in one central location. I do keep some specific types of cleaners in other places (kitchen cleaners in the kitchen, laundry needs in the laundry room, and toilet cleaners under the sink in each bathroom), but everything else is in this one cleaning closet. It is now so easy to find whatever I am looking for, all in one place.

My cleaning closet also has slightly recessed shelves to accommodate the handles of my vacuum, brooms, etc. I don't have much stored on the floor under the bottom shelf so that I can slide my vacuum cleaner in there and the handle fits up against the recessed shelves perfectly so the door still closes easily. My cleaning closet is 4 feet wide by 16" deep, and seems ample for all my supplies to fit easily. I also keep spare paper towel rolls, my small tool box, and other things in this same closet so they are easy to find.

Custom storage. If you have any unique storage needs related to your specific hobbies or interests, you may want to design in some custom storage areas in certain places in your dream house. Your household organization and quality of life are greatly enhanced by customizing your living quarters in this way. One caution, though, is that cabinetry is very expensive. If you can accommodate those needs by less expensive ready-made storage units, go for it. I just really wanted all mine built in and permanent.

In our old house, when we added on, I had our builder make me a custom cabinet with bookshelves above it all the way across one wall in our sunroom. The base of this cabinet was two feet deep, like kitchen cabinets, and the upper part was all open bookshelves of 12" deep. He also built me a very deep storage closet with hooks and shelves for all our scouting materials and equipment. We had backpacks, camping equipment, books, and all kinds of gear to be stored. Obviously, we were scout leaders, and had accumulated lots of "stuff" related to boy and girl scouting over the years. This closet was a godsend! And we never had to ask, "Where is ___?" again because it was all right there!

This is the type of thing you can design into your home to make it custom to your needs and activities. We obviously no longer needed that type of storage here, in retirement, so did not duplicate that cabinet here. Besides, there really was no place for a built-in that large. Instead, I had our builder here build me some custom shelves and closed storage on either side of the fireplace in the living room, which I had always wanted. If you have a fireplace, don't forget to design an appropriate mantle area and trim as well.

I think a fireplace with built-in shelves on either side is very visually appealing, as well as being an efficient place to store books and knick-knacks. Our shelves flanking the fireplace have glass doors on the uppers and solid wood doors on the lower half. That way, I can store books and pretties dust-free behind the glass doors, and other visually unappealing items in the lower storage behind the solid doors.

This works great in theory, but is not what actually happened. The glass cabinets now house the DVR, DVD player, stereo tuner, speakers, and all the electrical connections for our surround sound and other high-tech gadgets. We can see the DVR and DVD player through the glass and access them with the remotes, yet they are not dust-catching eyesores sitting out on a stand or shelf. This works even better than what I had originally planned! You can use your imagination to design your own custom storage, and maybe even come up with better uses for it when all is said and done!

I also have large windows on both sides of the fireplace, next to the storage shelves, with atrium windows above them and window seats below. I would have liked to have built in floor to ceiling windows on the lake side, but they are so expensive that I thought it was better to have the additional storage and seating/sleeping area of the window seats under them. The window seats are 7 feet long by 18" deep, so they could conceivably sleep two more kids, if need be. I put all the DVD's, CD's, etc. in one window seat, and all the "Grandma Toys" in the other side. That way, when the great-grandchildren come, they know right where to go for the toys. I keep ageless, classic toys in there like legos, tinker toys, etc.

Another feature I would strongly suggest is recessed medicine cabinets above all bathroom sinks, and upper cabinets above all toilets. In our half bath, we keep all first aid supplies, band-aids, etc. in the medicine cabinet above the sink. I put all the old ace bandages, slings, knee braces, etc., that we have accumulated over the years in the cabinet above the toilet so we can find them if a need arises. That way, it is handy for anyone to access and even "company" can get to it without going into your private areas. Since there is no shower or bath in there, it does not need the storage space for as many toiletries and makes a perfect place for first aid items. Each bathroom also has uppers above the toilet for toiletries, etc. Again, you can never have too much storage! And if you have it in a variety of places, it makes it easier for everything in your house to have a "home".

The way our vaulted ceiling and beams are arranged, I was able to add a plate rack along a beam in the dining room for my mom's collection of Danish Christmas plates. That was an afterthought, but I am so glad I came up with it before the construction was completed. It cost very little while they were finishing everything else, but would have cost a lot more if I had someone come back just to do that.

China cabinet &/or buffet. Instead of the wall-to-wall storage cabinet and bookshelves I designed for the sunroom in our last house, I designed a custom wall-to-wall china cabinet for my dining room here. Believe it or not, it was cheaper to have this cabinet custom built by our cabinet maker than it would have been to buy a ready-made china cabinet of the same size and style!

I designed my china cabinet with base cabinets much like a kitchen cabinet, to double as a buffet. Then I put uppers with lighted glass shelves in the center section for displaying my fine china and crystal. The lower, closed cabinet is for dining table linens, placemats, and more functional items like the fondue pot, etc.

On each end of this china cabinet, I designed floor to ceiling cabinets for closed storage more like small closets with adjustable shelves. This versatile storage space can be used for anything, since it is closed. In the right side cabinet, I have stored all my other "good" dining items (plates, cups, serving pieces, etc.) that are not as pretty as my formal fine china. These needed to have a home in the dining room, but were not pretty enough to be displayed like the china and other "pretties".

In the cabinet on the left side, I have stored all my family photos, albums and scrapbooking materials. I know that doesn't sound appropriate for a china cabinet, but the dining room table is where I plan to work on all that stuff. The china cabinet was obviously not designed for that purpose, but I had nothing else that needed to be stored in there, so why not? I had the space, and it accommodated that need perfectly, so that's what I did! It works great for keeping all that stuff in one location. And no one knows it's there because it's behind beautiful closed china cabinet doors when I'm not working on it!

Bookshelves. You may want to design some built-in bookshelves or other storage for kids' toys, etc. in strategic places around your home. Or, you may find much less-expensive bookshelves in retail stores. Whichever you prefer, be sure to plan what and where you will need this type of storage and allow space for it in your designs. If you have a home office, you may want a whole wall of shelves. Or, you may want to build shelves into a corner in your child's bedroom. I must say, though, that built-in storage does limit the way that a room can be arranged or used, so be sure to give it enough thought before you decide.

I put a small bookshelf in one corner of our game room that is perfect for our needs. It has, again, open shelves in the upper section and closed storage in the lower section. The upper section is perfect for our set of encyclopedias, some of our favorite hardcover books for display, and some "pretties". Then the lower section is used for DVD's, video games, and board games. This works great for us. You must determine how much of this type of space is best for you.

One decorating class I took suggested, for bookshelves to look best, they should be filled with: 1/3 books, 1/3 pretties, and 1/3 air. I have used this rule frequently and have been pleased with the results. However, if you have a lot of books, the shelves will obviously be full of books! Again, there is no hard and fast rule.

Laundry cabinets and linens. I think I covered laundry cabinets sufficiently in chapter 11, including my (not yet patented) sorting cabinet. I hope you will get some good ideas for designing your space from some of the suggestions I included there. As far as linens, I mentioned (also in chapter 11) that you should plan for a linen cabinet in each bathroom. In two of our homes, we had a linen closet in the bedroom hallway, outside the bathroom. This worked ok, but I really prefer to store mine in the bathroom where they are used.

Closets. Wood built-ins in all your closets are very expensive compared to the wire kits you can buy at retail. However, I cannot stand the wire kits! I had to have real wood shelves and storage in all of my closets, which also added to our over-budget total cost. But I absolutely love them! You can get wood kits as well in home improvement stores, and organize a pretty nice closet with them. Again, it's all up to you. If your closets are custom built, however, you can design every bit of storage space exactly as you want it.

I had my builder's carpenter build traditional wood shelving into all my closets and was able to custom design each one. From how far apart each shelf was, to how much hanging space was available, I got to decide exactly what I wanted in all of them. I had already designed what size and how deep each closet was to be, so why not finish the job? In some, I put shelves running up the sides of the closet, floor to ceiling, with a hanging bar only in the middle. In the guest bedrooms, my closets are 24" deep (inside) by 5 feet long, with shelves up one side and a shelf above the hanging bar.

In my master closet (approximately 10' by 12'), I made my side of the closet about one-third of it with a single bar for hanging dresses and nightgowns, and about two-thirds of it with double bars for tops and pants. On my husband's side, it is all double-bar for shirts, jackets and pants (he doesn't own many long dresses!). I also added floor to ceiling shelves on both ends on his side of the closet – one end for me and one for him - for folded clothes, shoes, etc. I put shelves above the hanging clothes on both sides for purses, suitcases, blankets, etc.

Walk-in closets come in all shapes and sizes, but mine is just a straight walk-through with clothes on each side, kind of like a hallway. It really is wider than it needs to be by about 2 feet. I could have done just fine with an 8 foot wide closet. But since it also acts as a pass-through to the laundry room, it is nice to have it a little wider. That also leaves plenty of room for clean laundry baskets waiting to be hung up or put away. Who is going to see those in my closet?

I have seen some houses that do not have walk-in closets at all, but instead they have one whole wall of built-in cabinets, probably around 24" deep. This wall of cabinets has a variety of different sized doors and drawers built in to hold different items. Behind some of these doors are hanging bars, whereas others have shelves or drawers. This is similar to a closet organizer, except it is not in the closet and all is behind closed doors within the bedroom itself. If you think about it, this kind of set-up may give you more storage per square foot because you do not need space to actually walk into the closet.

The following illustration shows what a built-in storage wall in your bedroom might look like, in lieu of a closet.

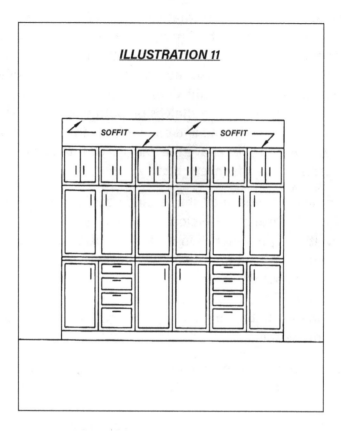

ILLUSTRATION 11

The only problem with a wall of built-ins is that it limits the use of that whole wall to just storage. This reduces your total wall space and may limit your options for furniture arrangement in the room. Whichever way you design your storage or closets, the important part is the total number of linear feet available for hanging space, and the total shelf space. Keep this in mind while designing, so you don't end up with a huge closet but not much actual hanging or storage space! I love my walk-in closet, but you may prefer a wall of built-in storage to give you more storage in less total space.

Last but not least, I think every house should have some kind of coat closet in or near the front entry way. It doesn't need to be too big, but it is nice to be able to hang up coats and jackets near the entry and close the door. In our old house, we had not only an entry closet, but a decorative hook assembly on the wall and an oak "hall tree". We also had hooks in the utility room just inside the garage door for coats and jackets there as well. The combination of all that worked well for us. Here, I still have the oak hall tree and a very small entry closet, but there are fewer people living here now so it is (barely) sufficient. I also have a row of hooks just inside the back door from the garage for jackets as well.

Speaking of just inside the back door, another suggestion for organization is a row of hooks on the wall, near the family's primary entrance, for hanging keys. I have a row of small decorative key hooks just inside the garage door entrance for car keys, golf cart, lawn tractor, etc. This works great and we can (usually) find our keys when we need them!

Custom cabinetry and storage is expensive, but I think it makes a big difference in your satisfaction with your dream home. And sometimes, the custom cabinetry may be less expensive than purchasing an equivalent piece of high end free-standing furniture. Therefore, this is another area you may need to check out when deciding what to build. You must choose whether you want built-ins versus free-standing furniture for storage. Just be sure to design in enough space for whichever type of storage you choose.

CHAPTER THIRTEEN

DÉCOR/DESIGN/COLOR/ FINISHING

I talked about much of this information previously, but there are so many more choices and decisions under this heading than you could possibly anticipate, so it's worth reviewing. And the more of these choices you can make before beginning the actual building process, the better. Of course, you may change your mind as the process goes along. But if you have already looked at the options, a second trip to be sure of your choices is a lot less time consuming than if you hadn't been at all. Building materials, textures, color, light, reflectivity, etc., must all be considered when choosing your décor and finishing details. Let's start with what comes first in the construction phase of the process.

Choosing your décor. Building materials are obviously the first choice. Most houses are built with wood framing on a concrete foundation. However, there are those that use metal studs or concrete blocks as building materials. Your geographic location may also play a part in what you choose or what local codes dictate. Going green may also influence your decisions here. I don't have a strong opinion on the alternatives to traditional wood and concrete, but you might want to consider your options. The building materials you choose will obviously affect the visual impact your whole house makes on first impression. Please see Chapter 6 on building and materials.

Your builder will probably have some options for merchants he uses and trusts. Sometimes your builder may get a discount from certain vendors he does a lot of business with. If he passes those savings on to you, the customer, it would be prudent to use the vendors your builder recommends. If not, I have no problem with any of the hardware or home improvement type stores you choose to look at.

Probably the first decorative choice you will need to make once the house starts taking shape is the roofing material. There are many choices in roofing color, texture, cost, and materials used, so be prepared to spend some time looking at samples and asking questions about the life, durability, fire safety, etc. of the varied choices out there.

Once you decide on roofing materials and color, you should probably choose your brick, stone or siding for the outside walls, as these two materials obviously need to complement each other. You may want to choose your siding material first and then choose the roof, but they do need to look good together. In choosing color, remember that darker colors absorb heat and lighter colors reflect it. This may make a difference in what you choose, as well.

Natural stone is probably the most expensive for your outside walls, but there are many man-made faux stone designs out there that are really beautiful. Just be sure and ask about weathering and insulation qualities before you choose. Brick was our choice, but I would have gone with natural stone if we'd had more money to spend. I am very happy with our choice of brick, and I think it goes beautifully with our natural surroundings, which was important to us when we were narrowing down the choices.

If you choose wood siding, remember that it will need to be re-stained and sealed or painted every 3 to 5 years. That is why we chose brick. With our age and retirement income, we did not want to have to worry about maintaining whatever exterior surface we chose. There are also many other options in siding besides wood. Vinyl, polymers, metal, and concrete board are just a few of the options out there. It is up to you to decide which material you want to go with. But again, be sure to do your homework on durability, weathering, maintenance, and cost before making your final decision.

Doors and windows would probably be next. However, since they have their own chapter (8), I will not waste much time discussing them. I do want to reiterate though, that size, style, color and choice of material will have a huge impact on your overall décor, from both the inside and the outside of your house. So choose wisely and take your time to get just what you want.

Appliances should be selected fairly early in the process, as their size and dimensions need to be decided before the cabinetry can be designed. Be prepared to have this information available for your builder when you are asked. Most people seem to want stainless appliances, but they do show fingerprints and streaks, so you may want to look at all the options before deciding.

Once you pick out your appliances, be sure and write down the model number and all specifications so your builder can have the exact dimensions of cut-out spaces needed for each. Your builder/ carpenter crew will need this information to allow sufficient space to install all your appliances. Don't forget to pick out everything you want included, such as refrigerator, oven/range/cook-top, microwave, dishwasher, washer and dryer, etc. An added note here: some of your appliances are usually NOT included in the construction budget, so you should plan your spending accordingly. You washer, dryer, and refrigerator may not be included in your builder's overall budget.

Next comes all your plumbing fixtures, faucets, sinks, tubs, shower surrounds, tile, etc. I really enjoyed shopping for all my water faucets, as there are so many more decorative choices out there than there used to be. You can really make a statement with whatever plumbing fixtures you choose. The new beautiful sink bowls that sit on top of the vanity are awesome, but I went with more traditional sinks for my house. My bathrooms are more functional than decorative statements, but I still think they are very appealing for my tastes.

I really want to caution you here. I paid WAY too much for my master bath spa tub. I wanted a million jets, and most tubs only had 4 to 8. I ended up with 12, just for the back, and 6 more for the rest of the tub. Because I have so many jets for the back, I have very little pressure there from each one. I think I would get a better back massage with only 2 to 4 jets in that area. I wish someone had told me this when I was shopping for bathtubs! I think 2 at the foot end, 2 on each side, and 2 to 4 at the back end would be the MOST you would want, for a max of 8. And if your tub is round or anything other than rectangular, I think 4 to 6 jets would be sufficient to address whatever needs you have. If I had known that, I could have saved thousands on my cast iron spa tub! I addressed much of the bathroom in a separate chapter, so don't think I need to spend any more time on that.

Next is floor and wall coverings, tile, wood, carpet, etc. I also have a caution here. I had picked out a really awesome tile for my master bathroom, but didn't think it went well with the vanity top I had chosen. So I changed the tile I was going to use on my master bathroom floor to something much more plain and traditional. I am so sorry I did that! The tile I had chosen was exactly what I wanted, but I ended up changing my mind at the last minute. It turns out that I liked that tile better than I liked the vanity top once it was installed, and wished I had changed the vanity top instead of my wonderful tile that I had picked out! It all turned out fine, but I do wish I had thought a little longer about this choice before deciding. In hindsight, I spent plenty of time on the layout, but not enough on the actual finishing touches and décor choices before we started building.

I guess there will always be some regrets, since you don't really know exactly how it will look until it is installed. I would just suggest that you ask as many people's opinions as possible to help you make those final decisions! I still love everything about my dream home, but would have done a few things differently, even after all the time I took designing it! That's another reason why I caution you to make as many of these types of decisions as possible before you break ground, so you don't have to make quick decisions that you may later regret.

Back to the flooring. Whether you prefer hardwood, carpet, tile, stained concrete, or other finishes, be sure to ask others about what they like/dislike about their choices. Most people today claim they want hardwood floors, but may not be familiar with how much upkeep it takes to keep them looking good. And stained concrete is awesome but can be slippery when wet. I am partial to porcelain tile or travertine, but they are very hard surfaces, so may not be the right choice for you. I also want carpet in my bedrooms because it is so much softer and warmer. Everyone is different. Just be sure you know why you are making the choices you are making, not just going with whatever is "in" right now.

Color, contrast, stain and trim. Paint and stain for your walls, cabinets and trim are probably next in your line of choices. First of all, what materials did you decide on for your interior walls – paint? Wood? Stone? Tile? Glass? Do you want some texture on your walls before painting them? I would strongly suggest some type of texture on your painted walls, but there are numerous choices. A wall that has no texture on it to me is very ugly. Hopefully, you will have a painter knowledgeable enough to steer you in the right direction on this.

You will also have to choose your wood trim around the inside of all your doors and windows, and if you want crown molding, etc. Your "finish" carpenter will help you choose these. We had one guy that did the finish carpentry but another person who did the staining. They are two separate steps. One is choosing the shape, depth and style of your trim, and the other is choosing the stain or paint color.

Do you want your trim to contrast with your wall color, or blend in smoothly? Do you want stained wood trim, or painted? It may take some time to choose your colors, so be sure and start early on these. I wanted some specific colors in my master bedroom, kitchen and family room. But for the rest I went with a soft neutral beige, and am very happy with it. There are so many beautiful shades out there to choose from now, so happy hunting! If you are unsure, I would go with the more neutral shades, either in a beige or a gray.

Next, you must choose your ceiling texture and color. All of my regular ceilings are painted white, but you can go with whatever you think best represents your tastes. Our cedar ceilings are really gorgeous, but quite expensive. Thank goodness we only put them in part of the house!

Other choices include cabinets, countertops, vanities, switch covers, hardware such as drawer pulls and towel bars, etc. I think I covered most of those choices in previous chapters. Just remember that there are so many tedious details to cover, be sure and allow enough time to find what you really want! Lastly, your furniture and art selections will finish off your décor.

Furniture and art pieces. We used mostly the furniture we already had from our previous house, but you may want to get some new pieces for your new dream home. Most people can't afford all new furniture, so be careful in selecting any new pieces to be sure that they will go with the rest of what you already have. We both fell in love with a beautiful wood (log) bed in a showroom, and came too close to buying it before we realized that if we got it, we would have to replace all the rest of our existing bedroom furniture for it to look right. Much as I loved that bed, I knew we couldn't afford to buy a whole new bedroom set. So we resisted the temptation.

When choosing what furniture you want to put where, just remember to leave lots of air space! You want to be able to move around your home easily and comfortably, and don't want every square inch of wall space covered with furniture! My game room here was originally crammed with furniture and very cluttered. When my daughter moved out, she took some of our (and her) furniture with her. That lessened the total amount of furniture in the game room and made a dramatic difference. Spreading the remaining furniture out around the room not only improved the visual appeal of the room in general, but the additional amount of light wall color showing made the whole room seem bigger, lighter and more pleasant.

I am not an interior designer! But I would suggest, as you place furniture, art, and accessories around each room, that you consider how each piece affects others in its vicinity. Instead of just slapping a picture or painting on a wall, try to group things artistically. For example, a chair, end table, lamp, vase, and wall hanging can make a pleasant impact all together as a grouping, instead of all separate pieces spread around. When placing a painting above a sofa, for instance, you should also take into account any end tables, lamps, and knick-knacks around the sofa and their impact on the whole grouping.

Picture height should usually be at eye level or slightly below, and look proportionate to whatever is under or around it. A small wall hanging would look out of place above a huge overstuffed sofa. A huge painting would overwhelm a small wall. Too much or too little wall space between the bottom of a painting and the back of the sofa will not look as good as "just right".

If you do not have any experience in this area, you can either hire a designer to do the whole thing, or even just pay a consultant for ideas to help you do it yourself. Sometimes, a friend's opinion can help a lot, too. And whatever you come up with can always be changed or re-arranged periodically. It took me three tries at wall groupings before I was happy with the way my game room was arranged.

Any particular grouping on a wall or in a room also has some "movement" to it, by the way the eye travels around it, so you need to take that into account, as well. I have heard of people putting the art pieces on the floor to get an idea of how to arrange them before putting them up. That can help, too.

Finishing. Once the house is built and the construction over, there will be lots of last minute finishing left to do before you move in. One is cleaning all the windows, doors and appliance surfaces. These will usually have stickers on them that must be removed, plus the soil and smudges that will naturally occur during the building and installation process. Both of my builders, here and in Oklahoma, had a professional cleaning crew that cleaned everything up before turning it over to us.

Cabinets and woodwork, flooring and plumbing fixtures must be cleaned, too. Even brand new appliances will have smudges and dust on them. And stainless appliances will show everything that has happened to them since the packaging came off! Your cabinets, countertops, and even inside your new shelves will also need to be dusted. Who'd a thunk I would need to dust INSIDE my new kitchen cabinets!?! Well, I did! Every surface, even flooring, will need to be cleaned from the construction dust and debris before you actually move in. Hopefully, that will be part of your builder's usual routine. But if not, you will need to do it or hire it done.

CHAPTER FOURTEEN
GARAGE, PORCHES, AND OUTSIDE AREAS

M ost people want at least a two-car garage, but some may want a three-car or more. The garage square footage is usually much less expensive per foot to build than the rest of the house because it has fewer finishes, little or no plumbing, etc. But if you design a very large or unique space, it can add up. You should have a definite building site in mind before placing your garage in relation to the rest of the floor plan, because your site may dictate where your driveway and garage should go. By the time you finish designing your house, you will probably have a good idea what your yard will look like. But it is still a good idea to give it some thought while you are designing the house. Your lot/building site can make a big difference in how you put it all together.

The garage and driveway. Our garage is an oversized two-car garage with nine foot doors so that any type of car or truck would easily fit in there. It is also deeper and wider than needed to allow for lots of storage along the sides, wheelchair access around both cars if ever needed, and a workshop area in the front of the garage. I also added 2 X 8 "backing" (mostly scrap lumber) behind the sheet rock on the garage walls at about 60" high for hanging storage units or anything else we might want to put up on the walls in the future. This backing will assure that the walls can hold the weight of whatever we want to hang on them. I did the same in some of my rooms inside as well, where I knew I would be hanging heavy pictures, mirrors, towel rods, etc.

How many cars will you need space for? How much parking room for guests? Would you prefer a carport to a garage? And how many cars, boats, motorcycles, golf carts, etc., will you want garage space for? How will you access the house with an arm load of groceries? What types of weather do you need to consider in your area when coming in from the garage? Will you have an attached garage? Detached? You really can design your garage the same as any other part of the house, and should think about your needs when doing so. Do you need space for a deep freeze? Storage cabinets? Tools? Yard implements?

Your road or street frontage may dictate where your driveway enters your property. If not, the location of your garage in your layout will determine where the driveway goes. Your driveway is an important consideration to the overall design, depending on where you live and if you have children. I loved having a circle drive growing up, but haven't had a lot that would lend itself to that since I was a kid. If you have preteens or teenagers, you may want a flat and large enough driveway for the kids to play basketball. If you have younger kids, you may want space for riding toys or skates. Or you may just need a single, straight-shot driveway into the garage. Some people may prefer the garage entrance to be around the side of the house, or even in the back. Others may not need a garage at all.

When planning your driveway, don't forget that concrete is expensive. The shorter and more efficient your driveway is, the less it will cost. However, you also want it large enough to provide sufficient parking for your needs. And be sure to design it wide enough to get in and out of the car without stepping in a mud puddle, wet grass or snow (for those times that you do not park in the garage).

I added a concrete pad in front of the house for extra parking, and to use as a turnaround. That way, we can back out of the garage to that direction and pull out of the driveway going forward, since the driveway and road are curved.

I also made our driveway as flat as was possible with the lay of the land (thinking of getting out when it's icy), but also sloping off to the side enough that water coming into our house was not going to be a problem. If you have very much slope to your lot, your builder should take water drainage into account before you ever turn the first shovel. You don't want water coming in anywhere in one of those flash flood events, so you should plan for the worst case scenario in your water drainage plans.

Porches, decks, balconies, patios. Porches, decks, balconies, and patios can add a great deal of visual appeal to any structure, so be sure to consider these in your design. A well-planned porch, deck or patio can also extend your living space by a considerable amount. Many people even incorporate an outdoor kitchen in their plans. A balcony outside your master bedroom may also be something you want to consider. When designing any outdoor spaces, be sure to take into account your view, neighbors, prevailing wind, sun direction, and access from inside the house. Do you want your outdoor spaces off the living or family room? Kitchen? Basement? Your house shape may also dictate this space and how protected it is from weather and public view.

I find that outside space where I can enjoy fresh air and nature is a real stress-buster. And a covered outdoor space is extra nice, so you don't have to worry about the hot sun or rain interfering with your morning coffee or an afternoon drink. And if you also have a screened-in space, you can enjoy it without the bugs! I absolutely love sitting on my covered, screened-in deck during a rain storm! It is so awesome to be able to enjoy my outdoor space without worrying about the weather. And I find being safe outdoors IN a rain storm to be electrifying, but maybe I'm just weird. I love thunderstorms as long as they are not severe, and if all my loved ones are home safe and not out in it.

I have ceiling fans on my covered deck for hot weather, and a table lamp heater for chilly nights and winter days. I use my deck as my "office" most of the year, because I love sitting out there more than anywhere else. Most days, winter and summer, you will find me on the deck doing my paperwork, paying bills, making phone calls, or whatever. My husband sits out there for hours, reading, with the dog at his feet, when the weather is nice. Retirement in your dream home is AWESOME! Just be sure to plan what features will give you the greatest quality of life for your interests and life style.

Landscaping. As your crews are finishing up the construction, leveling your raw dirt in the yard is part of the process, as is bringing in top soil to finish it off. Once that is done, you can start on your landscape design. Your elevation drawings from your drafting firm, showing the outsides of the house, will usually have some landscaping sketched in. You may use that as a starting place, or if you feel creative, you can create your own design. You can also hire a landscape architect to make it a real showplace, if you have the money.

Gardening and yardwork are not my favorite hobbies, so I designed mine to be very simple. When the driveway was poured, I had a sketch of the yard to show the builder where I wanted driveway, sidewalk, and open areas without concrete for simple gardens. I had three small designated, contained garden areas where I did not want concrete poured around the front porch. I had them leave three rectangular gaps of bare dirt along the edge of the front porch, beside the sidewalk, and up to the front door so that I could plant some low shrubs and ornamentals. By having these three areas surrounded by my concrete drive, porch and sidewalk, I didn't have to have any kind of edging to separate them from the lawn. It worked out great.

In the area along the front porch, I put in some low shrubs to kind of "fence" the porch. It looks really nice that way. I also have a similar sized rectangle between the sidewalk and driveway with two small dogwood trees and some day lilies, so I have flowers there all summer. These concrete-surrounded gardens really cut down on the amount of weeds and grass that I have to pull out of the garden, and they are very low maintenance.

I do have one caution here, though. If you are going to plant trees in your yard, especially if the area will be very close to the house or concrete areas, be sure and leave enough room around the base of the tree for root growth. The "drip line" around a tree is the area shaded by its leaf spread at high noon. If your tree is young, this spread will be pretty small. But if it will be a large tree, like an oak or maple, for instance, the drip line when it matures will be very large. Therefore, the tree should not be planted any closer to the house or concrete than its expected drip line at maturity. If this caution is not followed, your foundation or concrete may become damaged by future root growth. You also will eventually have branches from that tree growing over your roof line or even into the side of your house, doing damage in the process. Decorative trees are a real plus to any landscaping plan, but you must take these cautions into account.

I did not think about this possible future damage when I planted my dogwood trees in my front yard. I'm sure I did not leave enough space for their roots as they mature. Not only will I have to address this at some point in the future, but the trees have a tough time surviving in dry spells. Duh! Most of the drip line is covered by concrete, so they do not get enough water, even when we do get enough rain! I sure wish I had known this before I finished my landscaping! Oh well, hindsight is always better than foresight, right? And another reason to consult the experts when designing your dream home!

The rest of our yard is just trees and grass, but I did have some ornamental shrubs added here and there to spruce up the color somewhat. I also planted a Maple tree on the West side of the driveway to help shade the house, and some crocuses, daffodils and tulips along the driveway border. I have not yet added shrubs along the sides of the house, but intend to someday do that, and that will enhance the outside of the house considerably. Any landscaping that you add will increase the value and curb appeal of your house substantially. And consulting the experts at any landscape or garden shop will let you know what types of plants will accomplish your decorating goals.

My goals are always what will give the most show for the least care, but that's just my preference. If you have the money, hiring a landscape architect may be worth it, as a professionally landscaped yard will add much visual appeal to your entire home. I am pretty simple when it comes to landscaping, so did not feel it a worthwhile expense. But many people may need the creative ideas of a professional to feel like their yard and garden display is more detailed. There are endless choices, so just go for it!

I'm sure that I have not thought of everything you need to consider when designing your "dream home", but I hope I have at least given you lots of suggestions and food for thought. Good luck and I hope you get as much pleasure and satisfaction out of your new home as we have.

CHAPTER FIFTEEN

REMODELLING

This chapter is for those who are contemplating remodeling an existing home instead of building from scratch. From my experience, adding a new addition to an existing home is more expensive per square foot than starting new. This is because you have to work around existing structures and utilities, so more care must be taken and access may be much more difficult, especially for big equipment.

If you choose to remodel an existing house, many of the same principles apply. If you have a good imagination, you can see the good "bones" in even the most run-down house. You can change almost anything about a house if you have "vision" and enough money. But the things you cannot change are what you must look for if buying a "fixer-upper". Obviously, you cannot change the location or views, so those must be your first priority.

If the foundation, wiring, and plumbing are good, you can change most anything else in the house to suit your tastes. If you are remodeling the house you are currently living in, have fun. If you are looking for a fixer-upper to renovate, I would start from the beginning of this book and consider all the same areas as if you were starting from scratch.

First, you find a house in a neighborhood that meets all your requirements, location, lay of the land, etc. Then look at the size, space and layout, trying to ignore the décor. That is the easiest part to change. If you really want to renovate, don't be too picky. The main thing you are looking at is the space, efficiency and layout. However, if you are not wanting to spend very much in the remodeling process, you must consider more expensive changes such as tile, countertops, etc. Paint is cheap compared to other areas, so try not to rule some place out just because of the colors of the walls.

In undertaking any remodel, whether it is in your current home or a new purchase, I would strongly suggest you use this entire book for the process. Some of it may not apply, but there is enough information included in its entirety to help you be more knowledgeable and realistic about what you are undertaking.

During your remodel, be prepared to be frustrated, stressed, and exhausted for an extended period of time if you plan on living in the house while you renovate it. Just being realistic. I hope you have the stomach for it, as it is a challenging undertaking. In an existing house, you never know what you are going to run into. But in customizing your surroundings, it can also be the most rewarding of experiences. I've been there, done that, got the beads (sorry, scouting reference)! The next and final chapter includes a copy of my floor plan and ordering information.

CHAPTER SIXTEEN

MY FLOOR PLAN

If I had it to do over, I would make some minor changes to my floor plan. I said previously that I regretted placing the half bath in my kitchen nook, thus giving up the space for a kitchen table. Looking at my floor plan on the next page, consider the kitchen pantry and mechanical closet in the garage. Since my CHA furnace ended up actually centered under the house instead of in the mechanical closet, I would do away with the mechanical closet all together.

I would put the ½ bath where the mechanical closet and pantry are located, and take a small part of that half bath for either a small pantry or a broom closet off the kitchen. There is another closet across from the kitchen bar that could be the pantry. I would put the water heater in the small coat closet between the dining room and kitchen, although that closet would need to be a little larger to accommodate the water heater. These revisions would make the water heater much more central to the whole house and allow eating space in the kitchen nook.

Other than the above revisions and the lighting I covered in chapter 7, I would do it all over again. Good luck designing your dream home! I guarantee it can be done in less than 25 years because I did it in 24 ¾ . And, writing this entire book only took me three years.

My "dream home" floor plan is included on the last page of this book. If you choose to use my floor plan instead of designing your own, feel free. If you want to order a set of engineering print building plans ("blueprints") for the following floor plan, you can save nearly all architectural/drafting fees. Building plans to include:

    1 copy of floor plan
    1 copy of foundation plan
    1 copy of electrical plan
    1 copy of roof line plan
    1 copy of elevations from all 4 sides

To order, please send a check or money order for $975.00 to:

    Jan Evans
    P.O. Box 491
    Shell Knob, MO. 65747

Please include your shipping address and phone #. You will be responsible for any other versions required by your builder, zoning regulations, and building codes in your local area. Any architect's office can provide these for you with a copy of my existing plans. Happy hunting (for your lot), delightful designing, blissful building and lots of long-term living in your new dream home to you and yours!

FLOOR PLAN FOR MY DREAM HOME

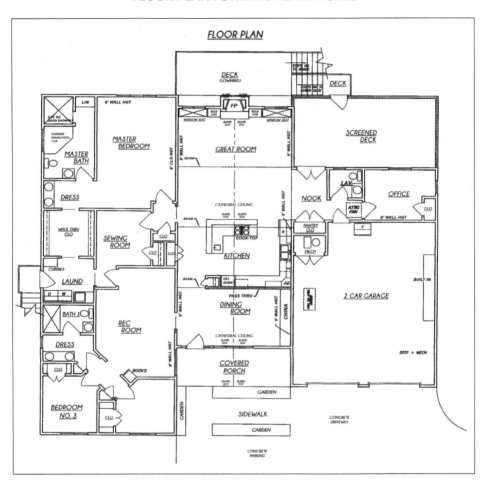

FLOOR PLAN

CPSIA information can be obtained
at www.ICGtesting.com
Printed in the USA
BVHW081059220822
645179BV00001B/66